Literary education:
a revaluation

Literary education:
a revaluation

JAMES GRIBBLE

CAMBRIDGE UNIVERSITY PRESS

Cambridge

London   New York   New Rochelle
Melbourne   Sydney

Published by the Press Syndicate of the University of Cambridge
The Pitt Building, Trumpington Street, Cambridge CB2 IRP
32 East 57th Street, New York, NY 10022, USA
296 Beaconsfield Parade, Middle Park, Melbourne 3206, Australia

First published 1983

Printed in Great Britain at the University Press, Cambridge

Library of Congress catalogue card number: 82–23527

British Library Cataloguing in Publication Data
Gribble, James
Literary education.
1. Literature – Study and teaching
I. Title
807 PN59

ISBN 0 521 25315 2 hard covers
ISBN 0 521 27308 0 paperback

For my students and my friends in the Dewdrop

Contents

Contents

Acknowledgements

I am grateful to the editors of the following journals for permission to use material I have published elsewhere : *Educational Philosophy and Theory, British Journal of Aesthetics, Journal of Philosophy of Education, Studies in Philosophy and Education, Educational Analysis, Journal of Aesthetic Education, Journal of Curriculum Studies, Journal of Education* (Nova Scotia).

I am also grateful to Professor P. H. Hirst for his contribution to the development of my interest in philosophical issues in literary education and to Professor S. L. Goldberg for his useful comments on an earlier version of the manuscript.

Literature, life and education: some problems about how they relate to one another

It is often assumed that if you assert with sufficient assurance and resonance that literature transforms our moral lives, or opens up worlds of vicarious experience through empathy, or leads to new vistas of knowledge and understanding of ourselves and other people, or educates our emotions, then that is all that is required. When a philosopher imprudently asks what all this means, or how it is known, he is likely to be met with hostility to such 'abstract' discussions of literary studies.

It must be admitted that there is some foundation for the wide-spread conviction, especially among university teachers of English, that philosophers lack genuine understanding of literary studies. Those philosophers who have taken an interest in literature are, typically, aestheticians, whose apparent lack of literary education is reflected in their failure to attend to literary works in an appreciative and discriminating manner. Very little philosophical work has appeared which exhibits an adequate understanding of literary criticism and scholarship.

A notable example of such work is John Casey's book *The Language of Criticism*.[1] It is not surprising that this has been out of print for a number of years. The hostility felt by literary academics towards such an enterprise by a philosopher is summed up in the reaction of one distinguished English teacher who refused to go further than the title, saying with great disdain, '*The* language of criticism, indeed!' If she had managed to overcome her prejudice against philosophy she would have found that Casey's book demonstrates a strong awareness of the richness and variety of critical language; but the stereotype of the philosopher trying to reduce critical discourse to narrow and rigid formulae remains a powerful one in the minds of many teachers of English in schools and universities. Partly as a consequence of this they go out of their way to avoid general (or 'abstract') discussion of the nature and point of literary education with either their students or their colleagues.[2]

This is an unusual situation, since there can be no doubt that in other subjects taught in schools and universities there has been a profitable interaction between subject teachers and philosophers. Philosophy of history has had considerable impact on history teachers at the tertiary level partly because of the challenge offered by the new discipline of sociology. Historians such as E. H. Carr and W. H. Walsh have been deeply involved in the analysis of historical explanation and of the distinctive concepts employed by historians. Educational theorists such as Burston and Perry have related this work to the teaching of history in schools. It is no longer so easy for history teachers to begin their work in schools without some serious discussion of the nature and point of the study of history. The 'New Mathematics' emerged from a break-down of the concepts and procedures employed by mathematicians and the implications of this for the teaching of mathematics even at the most elementary stages.

No comparable work has been attempted for teachers of literature. Instead, all too often, the teacher is met by a bewildering barrage of unsupported assertions, wild generalizations and pious hopes about the importance of literature in education.

Certainly no account of the point of reading and discussing literature would be complete without acknowledging that it is a pleasurable activity – a consideration which leads some proponents of a tough and rigorous education to be very suspicious of literature – how could it be educative *and* be fun?! And certainly no one should teach literature who finds no pleasure in it, although we have all come across literature teachers who dislike poetry but still 'teach' it. However, pleasure in reading and talking about books may be necessary, but it is not (as the philosopher puts it) sufficient to justify its significance in education or in life in general. There are plenty of pursuits which are undoubtedly pleasurable but which are of doubtful value or actually harmful – taking certain drugs, for example. And there are many, from Plato to the Pope, who maintain that literature can be harmful.

Introduction

It has always seemed to me that the most fascinating and awkward problems for readers and teachers of literature concern the relationship between literature and life. When I read *Crime and Punishment* or *Four Quartets* or see *Antony and Cleopatra* I am 'moved' in various ways, I have experiences of 'insight', I feel I 'know' more than I did before, I am involved in the 'lives' of fictional personages. And yet when I attempt to clarify to myself how these 'experiences', this 'knowledge', these 'feelings', this 'involvement' relate to my everyday experiences, knowledge, feelings and involvement, I rapidly become baffled and uncertain. In the intermission between the acts of *Antony and Cleopatra* I may talk with my friends about the powerfully moving experience of Antony and Cleopatra's passionate self-devouring, while at the same time drinking coffee, wondering whether the parking officer will book me for parking in a No Parking area and being rather taken with the appearance of the dark-haired girl in the corner of the foyer. After reading *Crime and Punishment* all night because my involvement with Raskolnikov is so intense, I shift effortlessly into the news in the morning paper and the bacon and eggs.

I don't think that these reactions of mine are atypical. The experiences of literature are connected in elusive and puzzling ways with those of everyday life. When we recommend a book to someone by saying that it will transform his view of marriage or comment that a poem offers a terrifying insight into our capacity for self-deception, do we really mean what we say? In what ways can literature affect our beliefs, our knowledge? What is the nature of our 'emotional' engagement with a work of literature? Such questions as these are rarely asked by most readers of literature, but they do seem to be ones which should be considered by teachers of literature in schools and universities. After a few years it may become very difficult to live with the very demanding job of teaching literary appreciation and discrimination with no way of articulating to oneself or others the *raison d'être* of the activity.

One factor which tends strongly to undermine the belief that reading literature might be of consequence for the way we view our lives and those of others is that it has become an examinable 'subject' taken by millions of students throughout the world. A B.B.C. television series called *The Glittering Prizes* contained an episode in which students trotted out, like shopping lists, phrases such as, 'indictment of our civilization', 'scarifying insight into our

3

secret selves', as comments on works of literature. The hollowness of such phrases suggested that it is frequently standard practice to offer large-sounding words to counterfeit the impact that the work of literature failed to make and that examiners frequently expect this.

It is generally taken for granted that if we are to teach geography or science or history, then it is of fundamental importance to examine the nature of the beliefs or knowledge which the children acquire, and to ask how these subjects may transform their way of seeing or understanding certain aspects of their experience. I was never much good at geology, but it certainly made some differences to the way I see various things. Sydney Harbour gains a new dimension once you learn that it is a drowned river system. Those twisted, wave-like curves in exposed rock-faces become intelligible once they are seen as the consequence of enormous pressures forcing the rock strata to concertina.

I have no doubt that *Crime and Punishment* and *Antony and Cleopatra* are much more important as ways of structuring and extending experience than my scraps of geology. And it is even, in a way, grotesque to ask what beliefs or knowledge are offered by such works of literature. But if such questions seem grotesque then we do need to try other ways of articulating the sense in which works of literature *do* extend our awareness or structure our experience.

Geology makes no demands on our feelings – we do not expect students to be particularly *moved* by geology. Literature teachers, on the other hand, do characteristically expect students to be moved by what they read. In fact they often claim that literature is an education of the emotions. Reference is often made to such notions as empathy, identification, or the vicarious experiences provided by works of literature. By 'feeling the feelings' of Raskolnikov or Humbert Humbert we allegedly extend our awareness of the possibilities of human life and this is said to be an affective rather than a cognitive matter. Such claims return us, however, to the puzzles about the nature of these 'involvements' with fictional personages and their connection with our involvements with people in everyday life.

On the other hand the literature teacher might be convinced that literature is morally educative, that literature offers positive life-enhancing values and reveals the inadequacy of lives dominated by greed, violence, lust, etc. Much literature does seem to be, as T. S. Eliot maintained, 'inescapably moral' in its implications, to be concerned with the way we should lead our lives or treat other people. In many schools, works of literature are used as adjuncts to social studies, and books allegedly 'about' old age, the environment, the family and so on are discussed. It is implicit in such courses that works of literature are viewed as sources of knowledge on matters of public or personal concern – I once knew someone who taught literature in a police academy who presented *Romeo and Juliet* as a study in juvenile delinquency!

Whether or not it is part of an author's intention that such implications are present is of course another matter and some would insist that it is essential to consider the writer's intention before making such claims. Ian Fleming may not have intended his readers to think that James Bond's character traits and pre-occupations are ones to be emulated, though the drivers of high-performance cars who buy 007 number plates seem to take it that way. What difference, if any, would it make if we found that Fleming had said that he did not intend, in the James Bond novels, to invite the reader to find it exciting to identify with a character who is violent, exploitative and ruthless?

Whatever answer we offer to this question, there is clearly a widespread belief that literature may be morally dangerous. For Plato this threat stemmed mainly from his belief that art presents deceptive but plausible images or appearances, and toys with the possibilities of evil in ways which lead them to be entertained because they become entertaining. More recently, such arguments have tended to narrow down to matters of sexual morality and violence. (In New Zealand, the film of James Joyce's *Ulysses* was shown to sexually segregated audiences, presumably on the grounds that its allegedly 'pornographic' impact would lead to the occurrence of immoral acts in cinemas!) Famous trials, such as that of *Lady Chatterley's Lover* in England and America and *Portnoy's Complaint* in Australia, reveal a wide spectrum of beliefs about the moral significance of literature. Many of the debates return to questions I have mentioned earlier, concerning the nature of our involvement with works of literature, the kinds of feeling they evoke, the extent to which knowledge and beliefs are offered in literature or received by readers; and, of course, the intentions of a writer can be of great consequence in a court of law.

Every now and then a dispute erupts in schools over a work of literature to which parents take exception and very often the same group of questions about literature are discussed. Such disputes are perennial because the questions do not seem to lead to any clear answers. This confusion is partly due to the fact that the issues overlap in so many ways. A debate concerning the moral significance of a book slides easily into arguments concerning the reader's feelings, or the extent to which the reader identifies with or empathizes with certain characters. The intention of a writer may be invoked to counter a charge of immoral persuasion and the 'truth to life' of a work may be advanced in defence of its portrayal of certain episodes.

I have bracketed all these issues together under the general heading of 'the relationship between literature and life'. My uncertainties about this relationship recur as soon as I take a step back from my immediate engagement with a work – and anyone who proposes to 'teach' a book ought to take such a step back and consider, however momentarily, questions such as : 'What knowledge or understanding, if any, have I gained from the work?'; 'Of what significance, if any, is the author's intention to my view of the work?'; 'What moral significance, if any, does the work possess?'; 'What kinds of feelings or emotions did I experience?'; 'How did my empathy for, or identification with, certain characters influence my response?'; 'In what way did the moral significance, emotional impact, etc., depend upon the (aesthetic) quality of the writing?'; 'What part does critical analysis play in determining the answers to any of these questions?' (or, 'Should I put my trust in my immediate reactions rather than my considered judgement?').

When such awkward questions as these get tangled up with one another I know that I am unlikely to come up with many straightforward answers. And yet my sense of the complexity of the issues which emerge when we ask, in these various ways, 'What is the relationship between literature and life?' is not shared by others who are interested in the teaching of English. On the contrary, many English teachers, critics and aestheticians appear to be in confident command of the answers to my questions. Many, in fact, think that the answers are so obvious that only a fool (or a philosopher) would be so tiresome or ignorant as to ask them.

I

Literature and truth

(a) Introduction

Where men are concerned I have always lacked a simple quality known as caution, or perhaps you might call it common sense. I meet a guy any other self-respecting woman would automatically run miles from and I manage to find something endearing about all his questionable characteristics, something rivetingly attractive about his manias. Adrian loved to hear this. Of course he excluded himself from the company of the other neurotics I had known. It never occurred to him that he was part of any pattern.

'I'm the only man you've ever met you can't categorize,' he said triumphantly. And then he waited for me to categorize the others. And I obliged. Oh, I knew I was making my life into a song-and-dance routine, a production number, a shaggy dog story, a sick joke, a *bit*. I thought of all the longing, the pain, the letters (sent and unsent), the crying jags, the telephone monologues, the suffering, the rationalizing, the analyzing which had gone into each of these relationships, each of these relation-dinghies, each of these relation-liners. I knew that the way I described them was a betrayal of their complexity, their humanity, their confusion. Life has no plot. It is far more interesting than anything you can say about it because language, by its very nature, orders things and life really has no order. Even those writers who respect the beautiful anarchy of life and try to get it all into their books, wind up making it seem much more ordered than it ever was and do not, finally, tell the truth. Because no writer can ever tell the truth about life, namely that it is much more interesting than any book. And no writer can tell the truth about people – which is that they are much more interesting than any *characters*.

'So stop philosophizing about bloody writing and tell me about your first husband,' Adrian said.

'O.K. O.K.'[1]

In this extract from Erica Jong's novel, *Fear of Flying*, Isadora, the narrator, reflects wryly on the connection between 'truth' in literature and 'truth' in life. The self-analysis of the first paragraph is exaggerated and flip – the self-mocking tone of voice reflects a fairly superficial cynicism about herself and suggests a 'pattern' in her relationships with men which falsifies because it ignores the complexities of her life. Initially we read it as inadequate self-analysis, until the sentence, 'Adrian loved to hear this'. We realize then that Isadora is aware of the inadequacy we have detected – that what she has told us is what Adrian loves to hear and, rather than being an introspective aside to the reader, her self-analysis is a summary of a line she runs with Adrian so that she can watch the way he laps it up, detach herself from him and privately mock his egocentrism. At least this is partly so. There is a self-defensive element in her strategy as well. And the put-down or 'placing' of Adrian in the last line of the paragraph implies some kind of acceptance of Adrian's categorizing : 'he was part of any pattern'.

Isadora then perorates on the relationship between 'truth' in literature and 'truth' in life, and initially this too sounds like direct communication with the reader. But she moves from the recognition that she has falsified her life in the telling of it to the generalization that no writer can tell the truth about life, and pontificates lamely that this truth is ('namely') that life is much more interesting than any book. We are made abruptly aware that this is not primarily an aside to the reader when Adrian interrupts – 'So stop philosophizing about bloody writing', and Isadora accepts the lameness of her generalizations – 'O.K., O.K.' Erica Jong skilfully leads us to think we're on a direct line to 'the meaning of the book', perhaps even the 'truth' that Erica Jong wants us to perceive, and then pulls the rug out from under our readiness to accept a facile commentary on the relationship between 'truth' in literature and 'truth' in life.

Perhaps to concentrate on the passage like this is to misread it, to treat Isadora as if she were the author and to treat entertaining, paradoxical play with the issue as if it were assertion and argument. It is such uncertainty about literary works to which Plato objected. Iris Murdoch has summarized Plato's condemnation of the artist in this way :

Art is sophistry, at best ironic *mimesis* whose fake 'truthfulness' is a subtle enemy of virtue. Indirectness and irony prevent the immediate relationship with truth which occurs in live discourse; art is thus the enemy of dialectic. Writing and painting introduce an extra distancing notation and by charm fix it in place. They create a barrier of imagery which arrests the mind, rigidifies the subject matter, and is defenceless against low clients. . . The art object cherishes its volubility, it cherishes itself not the truth, and wishes to be indestructible and eternal. Art makes us content with appearances, and by playing magically with particular images it steals the educational wonder of the world away from philosophy and confuses our sense of direction toward reality and our motives for discerning it. . . 'Form' thus becomes the enemy of knowledge. . . Form in art is for illusion and hides the true cosmic beauty and the hard real forms of necessity and causality, and blurs with fantasy the thought-provoking paradox. . . The true sense of reality as a feeling of joy is deceitfully imitated by the 'charm-joy' of art.[2]

Whereas philosophy and theology are obliged to reject evil in the course of explaining it, 'art is a shameless collaborator' and Plato 'rightly identifies irony and laughter as prime methods of collaboration'. Murdoch elaborates on Plato's position :

The judging mind of the skilful artist is a delicate self-effacing instrument; the tone or style by which the writer or painter puts himself 'in the clear' may be very close to a subtle insincerity. (As for instance in what critics call the 'placing' of characters in a novel.)[3]

Iris Murdoch is, unquestionably, a skilful artist. To what extent does her 'placing' of the characters in her own novels reveal her to be evasive in her presentation of moral dilemmas?

Consider, for example, the description of John Rainborough's sense of morality in her early novel, *The Flight from the Enchanter*. Rainborough 'knows' that he ought not to feel bitter and hostile because the council has confiscated the favourite part of his garden to make room for an extension of the neighbouring hospital's X-ray department.

When a well-meaning lady next door exclaimed to him that really, when you saw how much they needed the space, poor things, you couldn't be resentful any more, he replied with positive rudeness.
Rainborough . . . quietly deplored his attitude but left it to take its place in that ensemble of realities, a clear-sighted vision of which had lately come to serve him in the lieu of virtue. Self-knowledge, after all, was his ideal; and could not knowledge, by its own pure light, transform the meanest of discoveries? Rainborough did not feel that he was called upon, at his time of life, to put any more work into the development of his character than was required to provide a fairly minute commentary on how that development was in fact progressing. Actually to interfere with it did not enter his head. In moral matters, as in intellectual matters, Rainborough took the view that to be mature was to realize that most human effort inevitably ends in mediocrity and that all our admirations lead us at the last to the dreary knowledge that, such as we are, we ourselves represent the *elite*. The dreariness of this knowledge is only diminished by the fact that it is, after all, knowledge.[4]

Rainborough's jadedness is a product of his recognition that he is not able to *feel* towards the anonymous 'poor things' who will be treated in the new X-ray department sufficient sympathy to out-weigh the loss of his precious garden, and his refusal to disguise this from himself is something that he sees as a kind of virtue. Or *does* he see that his self-knowledge is 'in the *lieu* of virtue'? It is extremely difficult to determine the extent to which Iris Murdoch is drily placing Rainborough, in this passage, rather than Rain-borough wryly placing *himself*. Each of the ironies could be part of Rainborough's 'fairly minute commentary' on himself. The question, 'and could not knowledge, by its own pure light, trans-form the meanest of discoveries?' is a question which seems equally to be asked by both character and novelist. And whether either Rainborough or Murdoch believes that the dreariness of the con-clusion is diminished by 'the fact that it is, after all, knowledge' (or whether either of them *is* convinced that the conclusion *is* 'in fact' knowledge, or evidence of maturity) remains opaque.

But I do not think that this opaqueness is evidence of Iris Murdoch's evasiveness about moral matters. On the contrary I think that what she offers in this passage is a marvellous dramatiza-tion of an approach to morality or virtue that coherently sees self-knowledge as an over-riding value, which replaces or undermines 'goodness' in the conventional sense, but which in its attempt to be unillusioned cannot escape disillusionment (cf. T. S. Eliot's line, 'After such knowledge, what forgiveness?'). By allowing the pos-sibility that Rainborough is placing *himself* in this passage, Murdoch delicately avoids putting herself 'in the clear', as she would if she had distanced herself from Rainborough and, in the manner of the omnipotent novelist, detached herself from his ques-tions and left us with the impression that she could see through his self-deceptions.

The 'placing' of Isadora by Erica Jong, in *Fear of Flying*, does, by contrast, often amount to a subtle insincerity. It becomes very difficult to view Isadora through the various levels of self-aware-ness and self-deception, honesty and dishonesty to those in whom she confides. Erica Jong puts herself 'in the clear' by making her-self invisible behind the multi-faceted Isadora. Apparently a hard-hitting, ruthlessly honest book, it does 'cherish its volubility' and blur with irony (rather than fantasy) the thought-provoking para-dox. No novelist should be blamed for her publisher's blurb, but it is of interest that it is the 'truthfulness' of *Fear of Flying* which is stressed. The reader will 'be by turns blasted with the revelation of certain home truths which both men and women have been traditionally unwilling to acknowledge openly and convulsed with helpless laughter'. Any reader is promised 'revelatory new insights' into his or her own sexuality. On the contrary, however, it is more likely that the reader who becomes caught up in Isadora's fractured, confused sense of her sexual relationships would become more uncertain and confused about sexuality.

This is not necessarily to condemn *Fear of Flying* as a bad book, it is only to say that so far as 'truth' is concerned it is often evasive. Iris Murdoch maintains, against Plato, that every good play and novel is about 'the pilgrimage from appearance to reality'.

It is the task of mortals (as artists and men) to understand the necessary for the sake of the intelligible, to see in a pure just light the hardness of the real properties of the world, the effects of the wandering causes, why good purposes are checked and where the mystery of the random has to be accepted. It is not easy to do justice to this hardness and this randomness without either smoothing them over with fantasy or exaggerating them into (cynical) absurdity. Indeed 'the absurd' in art, often emerging as an attempt to defeat easy fantasy, may merely provide it with a sophisticated disguise.[5]

Fear of Flying has the highly sophisticated disguise of uninhibited frankness and honesty. Erica Jong is alert to many varieties of self-deception and pretension and Isadora sometimes pillories her own phoniness and that of others with ruthless accuracy. All too often, however, this descends to the level of Isadora saying to herself, 'Boy, are *you* stupid' (p. 272) or, 'I was nobody's baby now' (p. 244). She claims to have learned a lot from her 'real writing' : 'I started out being clever and superficial and dishonest. Gradually I got braver. Gradually I stopped trying to disguise myself. One by one I peeled off the masks; the ironic mask, the wise-guy mask, the mask of pseudo-sophistication, the mask of indifference.' This fails to convince, partly because the masks are not sufficiently distinguishable to be peeled off one by one. Irony is part of the wise-guy's repertoire and pseudo-sophistication is characteristic of ironic wise-guys. Isadora wants to believe that she is toughly confronting her 'true self' in her writing, as, by implication, does Erica Jong. But there is too little clarity, in such passages as this, for us to allow that the 'bravery' involved is much more than unearned self-congratulation.

Sometimes Erica Jong tries to suggest (through Isadora) that a writer's failure to get at the 'truth' or at 'reality' is inevitable, that language necessarily falsifies experience. On the other hand she also suggests that one reason why she writes is because it is through writing that she finds out the truth about herself : 'It is for this, partly, that I write. How can I know what I think unless I see what I write?'[6] This notion of writing as a process of identifying or discovering the truth about one's experience and 'inner life' has been given wide currency in discussions of children's writing as well as that of adults. Honesty, genuineness, sincerity, truth to experience are qualities to which English teachers are constantly encouraged to attend. In the final section of this chapter I will pursue further what is involved in this distinctively 'personal' conception of 'truth' as 'sincerity' in literature by following up D. W. Harding's ideas in his book *Experience into Words*.

The most commonly held view of what is meant by 'truth' in literature is, however, the accurate portrayal of aspects of the world or of human life. Many readers of literature believe that they gain knowledge and understanding from works of literature and would offer this as one of the reasons why reading works of literature is an important part of education. It is common to find literature courses in schools organized around themes such as 'the family', 'authority', 'race relations', etc., and some teacher education programmes include courses with titles such as 'Children in Literature'. One assumption of such courses is that the works of literature will develop knowledge and understanding of the nature of authority, the family, children and so on.[7] There is an expectation that a clearer perception of certain 'realities' will result. This may be thought to be a consequence of acquiring more information ('facts') about children or the workings of authority through literature, or it may be held that novels, plays and poems make us aware of larger, more general 'truths'. There is a familiar conception of 'truth' in literature here which is, to some extent at least, separable from the less widely discussed notion of 'truth' in the sense of 'sincerity' in literature. I will examine the more familiar notion first.

(b) **Truth and 'reality' in literature**

Small children often believe that the stories they are told are true, in the sense that the events related actually took place and the people in the stories actually existed. Later in childhood they become more adept at distinguishing fiction from fact, but they frequently retain an interest in true stories, regarding a book such as *The Dambusters* more highly than, say, *Biggles*, because it 'actually happened' and has 'true characters'. However it is rare to find adults who have had a 'literary education' expressing much interest in 'literal truth' in literature. Oddly enough, this is something that preoccupies those philosophers who discuss literature and the arts, the aestheticians.

There is widespread agreement among aestheticians that the 'truth' of a work of literature can only be construed as the relationship of its 'content' to observable fact. Sidney Zink's paper 'Poetry and truth',[8] for example, asserts that 'All statements claiming truth . . . involve a reference to existences outside themselves which they purport accurately to describe.' However Zink rejects the idea that literature could be true. 'Poetic statements involve no such reference, they describe nothing at all.' One of the most distinguished American writers on aesthetics finds it puzzling when sentences in literature refer to non-existent places, persons or things. 'A sentence about Huckleberry Finn or the green men of Mars is puzzling, for though it is about something there is no one for it to be about.'[9] One commentator wonders how anyone 'in their right mind' would think there is a puzzle here.[10] Indeed, the example demonstrates how far removed philosophers tend to be from the concerns of readers and writers, teachers and critics of literature. Their search for 'truth' in literature is a search for statements which are verifiable by empirical observation and investigation and they come up with the following examples:[11] 'The rainbow comes and goes' (Isenberg); 'I wandered lonely as a cloud' (Jessup); 'The warehouses of the Guild of Dyers were situated side by side with the Canonica of Or San Michele' (Beardsley). The inconsequential triviality of these 'truths' is acknowledged by some aestheticians but this does not lead to any questioning of the notion of 'truth' being employed. 'Whether the expressed truth is indeed a truth depends upon its correspondence with commonly observable facts' (Stolnitz).[12] Some aestheticians express an interest in generalizations they claim to elicit from literary works, for example, 'Love is an illusion which cannot bring us happiness' (Weitz),[13] and the morals of Aesop's fables, but Beardsley, who suggests the latter, says that the truths here are difficult to prove because they are so vague. The criterion of correspondence with observable fact reduces 'truth' in literature to bits of information. It is certainly not these scraps of 'facts' to which Iris Murdoch is referring when she writes of truth in literature as 'doing justice to the real properties of the world'.

Of rather more interest is the view, widely held among aestheticians, that when literary works contain predications they are not being *asserted* by the writer. That is to say, they are not truth *claims*, though they may be tested for truth or falsity. Literary works 'entertain' propositions rather than assert them. This suggestion has at least the merit of allowing some consideration of the tone or 'point-of-view' of a poem or a novel. Unfortunately it is usually elaborated in ways which re-establish the gap between the philosopher's interest in literature and that of teachers and critics of literature. For example, 'In the fictional use of sentences we simply pretend to refer or to talk about something.' The question of literature 'being about anything or its being true or false statement cannot properly arise'.[14] The literature teacher or critic will not be slow to point out that it is crass to say of any considerable novel or poem that it 'simply pretends' to talk about something or to deny that it is 'about anything'. We might say of the James Bond novels that Ian Fleming simply pretends to talk about sexuality and we might contrast them with *Fear of Flying* which is (at best) 'about' sexuality, in the sense that it sometimes accurately and honestly does justice to some aspects of the detail and complexity of human experience. (Compare the stereotyped fantasies of James Bond.) Of course, Isadora (and sometimes Erica Jong) 'pretends' – and sometimes pretends to pretend! ('Surely you don't think I'm telling the literal truth here, either?') But the point of such 'pretence' is to lead us to see the levels of pretence, to insist upon the possibility of self-deception and to contrast facile acceptance or self-delusion with those passages when an attempt is made to do justice to the real properties of the world and of human experience.

Only one or two aestheticians show any concern, in their discussions of truth in literature, with the distinctive ways in which poems and novels *work*. R. K. Elliott, for example, demonstrates that in an 'historical poem' by Cavafy it matters ('aesthetically') that there is reference to actual circumstances – this forms part of the way the poem works. But Elliott's conception of 'truth' remains firmly tied to references to actual circumstances or observable physical objects.[15] It requires a philosopher who is also a novelist to articulate a more adequate conception of 'truth' in art.

Perhaps in general art *proves* more than philosophy can. Familiarity with an art form and the development of taste is an education ... which involves the often largely instinctive, increasingly confident sorting out of what is good, what is pure, what is profoundly and justly imagined, what rings true, from what is trivial or shallow or in some way fake, self-indulgent, pretentious, sentimental, meretriciously obscure, and so on. Most derogatory critical terms imply some kind of falsehood. . . Bad art is a lie about the world. . . Strong agile realism, which is of course not photographic naturalism, the non-sentimental, non-meanly-personal imaginative grasp of the subject matter is something which can be recognised as value in all the arts, and it is this which gives that special unillusioned pleasure which is the liberating whiff of reality: when in high free play the creative mind is fixed upon its object. Of course art is playful, but its play is serious. . . Freud says that the opposite of play is not work but reality. This may be true of fantasy play but not of the playfulness of good art which delightedly seeks and reveals the real. . .

Art as the great universal informant is an obvious rival, not necessarily a hostile one, to philosophy and indeed to science, and Plato never did justice to the unique truth-conveying capacities of art. The good or even decent writer . . . attempts to understand and portray [other people's] 'worlds' and these pictures, however modest, of other 'worlds' are interesting and valuable. . . Art, especially literature, is a great hall of reflection where everything under the sun can be examined and considered. For this reason it is feared by dictators and by authoritarian moralists. . . The artist is a great informant, at least a gossip, at best a sage, and much loved in both roles. He lends to the elusive particular a local habitation and a name. . . Art is far and away the most educational thing we have, far more so than its rivals, philosophy and theology and science.[16]

It is hard to imagine how the aestheticians I have cited would respond to Iris Murdoch's claims. I think they would be most uneasy about a notion of 'proof' which relied on the development of taste and of 'confidence' in sorting out 'what rings true'. Even if they were to admit the narrowness of their conception of 'truth' they could, at least, insist that it is reliable. The contemplative, speculative aspects of literature should not be confused, in their account, with those respects in which it is true. For truth, they might say, you need more than a sensitive, well educated and discriminating nose probing for 'whiffs of reality'. How does one prove, to someone who thinks James Bond 'rings true', that it is trivial, shallow, fake and a lie about the world? What means are available to the literary critic to convince the sceptic of his perceptions of truth in literature which could compare with scientific 'proofs' through experiment and observation? These are questions which Iris Murdoch tends to gloss over but which must be tackled. In chapter 3 I will attempt to show that there are difficulties with the 'scientific' paradigm of 'objectivity' which are ignored by aestheticians. Determining the truth of propositions by examining their correspondence with 'observable fact' is by no means unproblematic, nor is it necessarily easier to meet the objections of those who are sceptical about such judgements than it is in the case of literary judgements. Before this comparison between the objectivity of empirical judgements and literary judgements is attempted, however, a great deal more needs to be said, both in this chapter and in the next, about the nature of literary judgements.

The aestheticians I have mentioned have a completely inadequate notion of what is the 'content' of a work of literature. There could be no point in examining the relationship between the 'content' of a work of literature and 'observable fact' if the nature of this 'content' is misconstrued. Aestheticians typically isolate 'poetic statements' or infer 'generalizations' from poems and novels without attending to a crucial characteristic of literary works, that 'what' is 'said' by them is intimately dependent on 'how' it is said. To use the jargon, 'content' is not separable from 'form' in literature. Some glimmer of this point is implicit in the view discussed earlier that works of literature 'entertain' propositions rather than 'assert' them. This is partly what Iris Murdoch has in mind when she refers to 'the playfulness of good art which delightedly seeks and reveals the real'. But most aestheticians fail to see that it is only through the distinctive *ways* in which works of literature entertain or 'play' with utterances that we can grasp 'what' they are saying. They fall back instead on the view that if literature does not 'assert' it must merely 'pretend' to assert or is 'not about' anything.

The inseparability of form and content in (good) literature is specified in this way by Matthew Arnold :

The superior character of truth and seriousness in the matter and substance of the best poetry, is inseparable from the superiority of diction and movement marking its style and manner. The two superiorities are closely related and are in steadfast proportion one to the other. So far as high poetic truth or seriousness are wanting to a poet's matter and substance, so far also, we may be sure, will a high poetic stamp of diction and movement be wanting to his style and manner. In proportion as this high stamp of diction and movement, again, is absent from a poet's style and manner, we shall find, also, that high poetic truth and seriousness are absent from his substance and matter.[17]

John Casey points out that this is 'one of the subtlest statements of the relation between form and content in literature ever made by a critic'.[18] It avoids the 'aestheticism' which comes from concentrating on the purely 'formal' aspects of literary works – a version of the aesthetician's claim that they are 'not about anything'. It also avoids the 'moralism' or 'didacticism' which is associated with attempts to judge the 'truth' of a work of literature separately from its form. Such moralism or didacticism is frequently to be found when children are encouraged to paraphrase the 'message' of a poem or a story or to identify what it is that the author is 'trying to say'. As if writers of good literature are peculiarly incapable of clear communication and find it necessary to dress up or obscure their 'meaning' with an ingenious array of verbal contrivances – a kind of puzzle for children to solve by guessing which answer the teacher has in mind.

Any attempt to give an account of the sense in which works of literature may be said to be true, or to lead to knowledge or understanding, would have to do justice to the subtleties of Arnold's statement and to the very great variety of ways in which works of literature reflect on (play with/entertain) human life and its concerns. The inseparability of form and content in literature does make it peculiarly difficult to 'formulate' our understanding of works of literature or the respects in which we claim them to be 'true'.

It is one of the main contentions of this book that literary criticism is that form of discourse which undertakes the analysis of works of literature so as to do justice to their 'embodiment' or 'realization' of meaning. In the next chapter I will discuss in some detail the nature of literary critical analysis and the means by which it may respect the 'organic' interaction of 'form' and 'content' in literary works. Before I defer the issue in this way, however, it might be of some use to offer an example of what I mean. I have selected a passage of poetry which is actually 'about' literary criticism. In fact it is a scathing attack on critics who *fail* to respect the complex interaction of the 'parts' in an 'organic whole'.

> The critic Eye, that microscope of Wit,
> Sees hairs and pores, examines bit by bit;
> How parts relate to parts, or they to whole,
> The body's harmony, the beaming soul,
> Are things which Kuster, Burman, Wasse shall see,
> When Man's whole frame is obvious to a flea.
> (*The Dunciad*, Book IV)

These lines illustrate one of the many ways in which literary works may be said to be 'organic' and to 'enact' or 'realize' their meaning.[19] So much, for example, depends on the semi-colon (line 2). The possibility remains, until the last line, that the critic eye does see, 'How parts relate to parts, or they to whole, / The body's harmony, the beaming soul'. There is, as it were, a 'double aspect' created by the syntax and the punctuation. 'The critic Eye . . . sees . . . how parts relate to parts'. But if this is so, 'are things' does not follow grammatically and 'shall see' makes us realize that the critic eye does not see the whole physical and spiritual organism that is man (or a poem). The penultimate 'see' drops us into the contemptuous cadence of the last line, and the rhyme with 'flea' recalls the hairs and pores which are all that the critic eye sees. The image of a flea on a human body is kept tacit until the final word, when we realize that the critic's is a 'flea's-eye-view' of literature.

The ostensible analogy, to begin with, is between the critic's view of a poem (as an 'organism') and the anatomist's or physiologist's view of a man (also as an 'organism'). The 'microscope' suggests scientific reliance on what is 'obvious' to perception, on what can be 'seen directly', lending an air of precision and 'objectivity'. Nevertheless, what can be seen is mediated through a lens which narrows the focus of what can be seen to 'hairs and pores'. The 'body's harmony' (suggesting, perhaps, the dimension to which Michelangelo's drawings of the human body in a circle draw attention) and the 'beaming soul' (the radiance of this vision is momentarily 'caught' by the word 'beaming', as is the hint of a smiling benevolent face) are 'seen' in a quite different sense. They are seen 'imaginatively' and such perceptions are implied to be inaccessible to those who peer through microscopes.

Pope's lines exhibit and 'enact' a number of 'insights' into, for example, bad criticism, the nature of literature and different modes of 'seeing'. The lines themselves dramatize the 'insights' to which they draw attention. They themselves compose an 'organism' and their 'meaning' is not separable from reading 'these words in these positions'.[20] Unless someone could give some kind of account of the lines which draws attention to such features as those I have noted (in particular, the 'ambiguity' or 'double aspect' of the lines) we would have no grounds for crediting that he understands the lines, let alone that he could judge or assess their 'truth'.

The conclusion I have come to (and it is only an interim conclusion) is that there is a question which is logically prior to questions about 'truth' in literature. This question is, 'How is literature to be understood?' The difficulty facing the philosopher who wishes to analyse the sense in which 'truth' may be attributed to a work of literature was suggested earlier in the passage from Matthew Arnold. I said then that any attempt to do justice to the sense in which works of literature may be said to be 'true' would have to attend to the subtleties of Arnold's statement and to the very great variety of ways in which works of literature reflect on human life and its concerns. A few of these have been referred to, by way of example, in connection with the lines from *The Dunciad* and the earlier extracts from *Fear of Flying*.

With literature, so much depends upon the *form* of words to be understood that the usual devices we employ to convey our understanding (re-casting, paraphrasing, etc.) are in many ways inadequate to the task of expressing and conveying our understanding of literary works and thus identifying the respects in which we might hold that they are true. It is with something like this in mind, I think, that Wittgenstein distinguishes between two 'uses' of 'understanding':

531. We speak of understanding a sentence in the sense in which it can be replaced by another which says the same; but also in the sense in which it cannot be replaced by any other. (Any more than one musical theme can be replaced by another.)

In the one case the thought in the sentence is something common to different sentences; in the other, something that is expressed only by these words in these positions (Understanding a poem).

532. Then has 'understanding' two different meanings here? – I would rather say that these kinds of use of 'understanding' make up its meaning, make up my *concept* of understanding.

For I *want* to apply the word 'understanding' to all this.

533. But in the second case, how can one explain the expression, transmit one's comprehension? Ask yourself: How does one *lead* anyone to comprehension of a poem or of a theme? The answer to this tells us how meaning is explained here.[21]

When literary works exhibit the intimate connection between form and content to which Wittgenstein refers (when 'what' is 'expressed' is expressed only by 'these words in these positions'), the usual methods of explaining and teaching for understanding are made inadequate. What has to be understood in such literature cannot be paraphrased and re-cast without loss of meaning, as was demonstrated in the discussion of Pope's lines. But this should not lead to a distinction between two kinds of 'understanding'. Understanding literature is not private, personal and inaccessible to teaching and testing. There are 'personal' elements in *all* forms of understanding. (One has always to 'see' connections for oneself, even in mathematics – no one else can do this for you, however well he might 'lead' you to see them.)

When meaning cannot be separated from the form of words in which it is expressed, distinctive techniques of teaching and testing are required. The process of leading someone towards the meaning of a work of literature (without losing sight of the way its meaning is 'embodied', 'enacted' or 'realized' in only 'these words in these positions') is the concern of literary criticism. It is a matter of pointing out aspects, re-directing attention to features of literary works which, when grasped, lead to an appropriate experience of the work. The activities of the critic and the teacher of literature are, in this way, closely bound up with one another.

Put like this, both criticism and teaching sound very one-sided. Whereas both activities should be collaborative. Teachers can learn from their pupils just as critics can learn from one another. Both are 'common pursuits' – the 'common pursuit of true judgement'. In the context of mass schooling this is easily lost sight of, unfortunately. Even in philosophy, which is not a 'school subject', the collaborative 'dialectic' which Plato valued so highly tends to become smothered under the pressure of exams, reading lists, lectures and text-books. Wittgenstein is reported to have said of one of the books he reluctantly published. 'This is not philosophy – you could learn it by heart!' Learning opinions by heart, in either literary criticism or philosophy, is, of course, death to both pursuits.

Our initial questions concerning the possibility of 'truth' in literature have, of necessity, given way to questions about how literary works are to be appropriately understood. If literature reflects 'reality' and has 'unique truth-conveying capacities', the 'reality' it reflects and the 'truths' it conveys are not accessible to those who, in their quest for snippets of empirically verifiable information, fail to see that 'what' is conveyed in a work of literature is not separable from 'how' it is conveyed.

Can literary criticism do justice to the distinctive ways in which literature 'works'? How can a critic demonstrate the 'appropriateness' of his understanding of a work of literature? Does the 'common pursuit of true judgement' concerning literary works actually lead to any true judgements? These are some of the questions to be considered in the next chapter.

(c) Truth and 'sincerity' in literature

Usually when we speak of finding words to express a thought we seem to mean that we have the thoughts rather close to formulation and use it to measure the adequacy of any possible phrasing that occurs to us, treating words as servants of the idea. 'Clothing a thought in language', whatever it means psychologically, seems a fair metaphorical description of most speaking and writing. Of Rosenberg's work it would be misleading. He – like many poets in some degree, one supposes – brought language to bear on the incipient thought at an earlier stage of its development. Instead of the emerging idea being racked slightly so as to fit a more familiar approximation of itself, and words found for *that,* Rosenberg let it manipulate words almost from the beginning, often without insisting on the controls of logic and intelligibility.[22]

In his discussion of Isaac Rosenberg's poetry, D. W. Harding suggests that the 'thought' in his poetry 'remains ungraspable – incapable of formulation in slightly different terms'. Harding contrasts this with 'acute conversation', in which highly differentiated ideas are presented through the most effective *illustration* that can be found. 'Rosenberg rarely or never illustrated his ideas by writing, he reached them through writing,' a process which Harding says is by no means usual in most writing and speaking.

At the end of section (a) of this chapter I drew attention to Erica Jong's suggestion that writing may be a form of self-discovery or of exploration into the 'truth' about one's experience or inner life. Isadora says, 'It is for this, partly, that I write. How can I know what I think unless I see what I write?' I expressed some doubts about whether or not Isadora's self-exploration gets very far. She strikes an attitude of ruthless honesty which is self-engrossed rather than self-exploratory. Nevertheless her *desire* to see herself as plumbing the depths of her thoughts, her experience, through her writing is part of a widespread contemporary admiration for qualities such as honesty, sincerity and 'truth to experience' in literature. English teachers, too, are expected to be highly attentive to these qualities in children's writing. D. W. Harding is one of the few writers who has attempted to develop an account of what is involved in referring to 'truth' in the sense of 'integrity' or 'sincerity' in literature.

Harding recognizes a quality in T. S. Eliot's poetry which is similar to that which he finds in Rosenberg's. 'Meaning', for Eliot, is 'what he intends his words to do' and this necessitates the 'difficult task of *not* saying something like it and more familiar'. This attempt to be 'true' to 'incipient thought-feelings' is unlike the 'ordinary way' in which we attempt to state the meaning by taking abstract ideas and piecing them together or illustrating them.[23] 'When something like this happens, and abstract concepts already available are being used', the tendency is 'towards generalization away from, rather than through, particularities of experience'. The 'genuine' (truthful/sincere/honest) writer strives to arrive at words which will complete and embody his experience without distortion. As Coleridge puts it, 'The word (for the Imagination) is not to convey merely what a certain thing is, but the very passion and all the circumstances which are conceived as constituting the perception of the thing by the person who used the word.'[24] The integrity or truthfulness of the writer is apparent if he does not skid into approximations, the tempting abstractions, the ready clichés of 'ordinary language or conversation' but embodies the 'concrete actualities of experience' in his words.[25]

But this separation between the movement of thought into 'genuine writing' and into 'ordinary speech' is seen by Harding to be basically factitious. After all, the writer does not always try to maintain the distinctive 'faithfulness to incipient thought-feelings', and he may try to do so but fail. And there are ways in which everyone may sometimes achieve some degree of faithfulness to the peculiarly personal quality of their own thoughts and experiences which Harding ignores. Before I draw attention to the ways in which the 'ordinary speaker' may make apparent the vividly personal, unparaphrasable dimensions of his 'thought-feelings' there are some complexities mentioned by Harding which must be considered.

In a single paragraph of *Experience into Words* Harding both contrasts 'experience' and 'words' and also points to two characteristics of their interaction in verbalizing:

Verbalising seems to be a two-sided process in which both sides are simultaneously active. On the one hand human experience includes an infinite variety of shades and patterns of feeling, attitude, desire, interest and discrimination. On the other hand language provides a vast range of subtle ways by which we refer to such experience. When we speak or write, experience in some ways merges with, and emerges in the form of patterns of language. But in some minds the language processes reflect not only the main experience, in statements that could be more or less paraphrased, but also much subtler features of the non-verbal experience, and features of which the writer may have had no awareness except through the overtones of what he finds himself writing. Even then he may fail to notice what he has said.[26]

The main difficulty here is the notion of non-verbal experience. Other formulations such as 'incipient thought-feelings' do not help much as clarifications. In fact it is not easy to clarify since it has to be discussed in terms of its manifestations, or 'indirectly'. Nevertheless, Harding offers us a useful distinction which, partly by letting us know what it is not, helps us to see what it is.

The non-verbal aspects of thought, the emergent definitions of interest, awareness of task or intention, perceptual discriminations, images, half-grasped similarities, shades and contrasts and conflicts of attitude, part-activated sentiments, suspected relevancies of information, *these are not to be called pre-verbal.* For in all probability language plays a part almost from the beginning of the process. Words are available, aiding definition or tempting towards distortion from the earliest stages of thinking; for many people they are promptly available as non-verbal [*not* pre-verbal] imagery. Far from serving merely to 'express' thought, they are one of its elements and a constituent part of the total pattern of inner behaviour that thinking is. In fact it may happen that the words emerging possess ambiguities or obscurities that preserve features of the inner behaviour denied by the intended statement.[27]

The extent to which a writer need be *aware* of the 'experience' which is embodied in his words is a consideration which must be deferred if the present issue is to be kept clear.[28] The main consideration at present is the way in which language interpenetrates 'experience', even that which is non-verbal, by acting as a kind of catalyst on the relatively undifferentiated matrix of feelings, intuitions, attitudes, etc. For all writers and speakers, 'words are available . . . from the earliest stages of thinking' or experiencing. But for the writer or speaker to exhibit integrity or 'truth to' his experience he must avoid the tempting distortions and capture in his words not merely 'the main experience, in statements that could be more or less paraphrased, but also much subtler features of the non-verbal experience'.

Harding's analysis returns us, by a different route, to the point with which I concluded the previous section. In conveying our understanding or appreciation of works of literature which achieve such 'truth to' the uniquely personal aspects of 'experience'[29] it will be essential to avoid reducing them to the 'more familiar approximations' which are so readily available. The 'temptations' towards cliché and stereotype, towards sentimentality and banality, which the writer may have avoided, often after great effort, are particularly dangerous for the teacher who is concerned to make a work of literature 'available' for students. By inviting students to treat a poem or a novel as a more-or-less elaborate or complicated way of saying something which could be put more simply or straightforwardly in other words, it is likely that they will be encouraged to ignore precisely those features which make it a significant achievement. Conveying one's understanding and appreciation of a work of literature which manages to achieve fidelity to delicacies and nuances of thought, feeling and attitude requires a form of discourse which has a high degree of tact and flexibility. At its best, literary critical discourse exhibits these characteristics, as I will suggest in the following chapter.

Before I turn to an examination of the nature of literary critical discourse, however, there is a further point I want to make about the 'ordinary speaker' or writer who, in Harding's account, is contrasted with the poet because he skids into facile approximations and fails to maintain a high degree of fidelity to the distinctively 'personal' and unique aspects of his 'experience'. I think it is worth observing that what the 'ordinary man' does not do in writing or by the *words* he uses in speaking, he can to some extent do by other means *as* he speaks. Unparaphrasable and subtle features of our 'non-verbal experience' are often captured in gesture, facial movement, hesitation, emphasis, intonation, rhythm and many other 'devices' which characteristically interact with our words to create meaning. There will be great variation, too, in the extent to which we are *aware* of this subtle counterpoint to our words, which makes them peculiarly personal and unique. I think they may be said to gain a kind of personal uniqueness, despite the fact that in *writing* the words may be crude approximations, appearing only as a paraphrasable stereotype.

I used the word 'device' a moment ago because it seemed to me to be inappropriate, and the best way of illustrating its inappropriateness was to use it in that context. For what are often called 'literary devices' are not tricks or contrived 'effects', any more than are those accompaniments to our words in conversation just mentioned. To develop the analogy, the equivalent of the 'pseudo' writer is the rhetorician – and he is, in a sense, a 'phoney' speaker. It may be just as inappropriate to say of the work of a 'genuine' writer that he 'uses literary devices' or 'creates effects' as it would to describe a genuine participant in a conversation in such ways.

I should make it clear that I am not proposing a simple contrast between 'deliberate contrivance' (equalling 'pseudo' literature or 'Fancy') and 'unconscious spontaneity' (equalling 'genuine' literature or 'Imagination'). There is a great range of possibilities between these extremes and most literature which offers a 'complex ordering of belief and attitude' will contain elements of both kinds of mental process. In the case of Shakespeare's plays, however, the relations between the images, the interpenetration of one image into another, the extraordinarily complex, 'organic' and effortless control over rhythm, movement, line-stop, metaphor, etc., could hardly have been deliberately contrived. Consider, for example, the shift in the half-activated image of the horse when Macbeth declares,

> I have no spur
> To prick the sides of my intent, but only
> Vaulting ambition, which o'erleaps itself,
> And falls on th'other [side]

The line-stop after 'only' gathers us for the ascent of 'vaulting ambition' and the final line falls flat in a heap. The half-articulated image of the horse shifts from one which is reluctant to one which is over-eager, reflecting the subterranean shifts and conflicts in Macbeth's mind. Such passages occur constantly in Shakespeare's plays and they exhibit Shakespeare's capacity to 'inhabit' the psychological states of his characters to the extent that the verse retains 'emergent' features of thought and feeling. It seems absurd to suggest that Shakespeare had a clearly defined notion of what he wanted Macbeth's words to illustrate and then set about finding the right words for it. Shakespeare's lines do not illustrate Macbeth's state of mind, they 'enact' and 'realize' it.

On the other hand it seems likely that Pope had a pretty clear idea of what he intended his words to do in his creation of the critic's 'flea's-eye-view' of literature. I argued earlier that these lines work 'organically', though I think this is the product of deliberate contrivance. (Rhetoricians may not be 'genuine' speakers, 'true to' their 'experience', but they may contrive brilliant and telling effects.) The 'double aspect' of the tacit image of the horse in the passage from *Macbeth* (both reluctant and too eager) is not deliberated as the 'double aspect' of the critic's-eye-view of literature seems to be contrived by Pope. But in both examples, only 'these words in these positions' could enact the meaning. Parts relate to parts, and they to whole in the final product, regardless of the apparent differences in the process of composition in each case.

I have argued that in ordinary conversation a speaker's use of intonation, gesture, rhythm, emphasis and so on may capture unparaphrasable and subtle features of his 'non-verbal experience', even though the *words* he uses fail to achieve 'truth to' his 'experience'. Harding points out that sometimes even the words we use may contribute to this.

The emergence of words or images as part of our total state of being is an obscure process, and their relation to the non-verbal is difficult to specify. They are not simply the expression of a state of mind; they are part of it. Even in ordinary conversation the phrasing of an attitude is sensitively keyed to the context in which we are speaking and – apart from polite concealments and hypocrisies – the phrasing we adopt is part of the attitude we find we have taken up.[30]

'Find' is the operative word here. Harding is directing attention to the way in which the words which occur to us may subtly develop our thought as we speak. When, in conversation, we narrate an experience (an incident at work or school, an encounter with an old friend, a film we have just seen) we are more or less aware of looking for words to fit the 'experience'. Often the words we use steer our attitudes or our state of mind into slightly un-expected channels – we 'find' we have taken up an attitude. The attitude we find we have taken up in the phrasing we adopt may approximate closely to aspects of our state of mind of which we were only partly, if at all, aware – we 'give ourselves away' in what we say, perhaps. (When Isadora concludes her 'put-down' of Adrian by saying, 'It never occurred to him that he was part of any pattern', we are aware that Isadora is acknowledging, in some part, an acceptance of Adrian's categorizing of her. It is of little consequence whether or not Erica Jong 'contrived the effect' – the duality is crisply 'realized'.)

It follows that R. P. Blackmur's account of the way language may act as a catalyst on the 'rich matrix' of non-verbal ordering of experience could be as true of the man in the street (or the child in the classroom) as of the novelist or poet. Blackmur is obviously thinking of the fact when he writes of his (the poet's) finding in his words a pre-existent reality, deeply ready and innately formed to give an objective being and specific idiom to what he knows and to what he does not know that he knows. But Harding does not get carried away, as some poet-critics do, by observations of this kind and he makes some important reservations.

To say this [that words are *part* of a state of mind] is not to accept the simple view of Watsonian behaviourism that thinking is indistinguish-able from sub-vocal speech. Against this is the common experience of trying unsuccessfully to phrase a complex state of mind, and having to say, 'No, that isn't quite what I mean'; when that happens the verbal formulation is evidently not fully consistent with some other non-verbal aspects of the discriminations and attitudes which are emerging, and we go on groping. At the other, and equally unacceptable extreme from the early behaviourist view lies the naive separation of thought from speech that led to the metaphor of finding words to clothe the thought, and to the ideal of writing, 'What oft was thought but ne'er so well expressed.' This latter view is unacceptable if it implies that there could be alternative phrasings of the same thought, but acceptable if it points to the ideal of finding one fully accurate and adequate expression of all that lurks within the thought.[31]

By insisting that it is 'unacceptable' to imply that there could be alternative phrasings of the same thought Harding is emphasizing something that Wittgenstein had in mind when he referred to sentences which 'cannot be replaced by any other', in which the thought is 'something that is expressed only by these words in these positions' (see above, p. 20). However Harding is ignoring Wittgenstein's other sense of 'understanding a sentence', in which 'we speak of understanding a sentence in which it can be replaced by another which says the same', in which 'the thought in the sentence is common to different sentences'. In many areas of discourse it is not the concern of the writer or the speaker to attend to their non-verbal discriminations and attitudes (or 'all that lurks within the thought') but to establish a point in an argument, to conclude a bargain, arbitrate a quarrel, get something done and so on. In what may be loosely called 'practical life' the effort in verbalizing is not to 'find one fully accurate and adequate expression of all that lurks within the thought'. Verbalizing is directed towards achieving an 'external' purpose – getting something done, demonstrating that something is the case – and words and sentences can be re-cast and paraphrased without significant loss of meaning, i.e. without impairing the effectiveness of the sentences for the purpose of 'conveying messages'.

The 'ideal' to which Harding refers, of 'finding one fully accurate and adequate expression of all that lurks within the thought', helps to correct the naive separation of thought from words which is implied in the eighteenth-century ideal of 'what oft was thought but ne'er so well expressed'. Radically separating 'form' from 'content', this ideal values the elegance and beauty of the author's *manner* of expression – good poets are good stylists. As well, good poems are not distinguished by the quality of their 'thought' since the truth (or wisdom or justice) of 'thought' is held to be independent of the words, the form in which they are expressed. A good poet cannot be distinguished by his 'ideas', his 'philosophy', since the ideas he expresses are commonplace.[32] In the previous section I argued that this 'ideal' is misconceived and Harding gives further support for the defence of Arnold's view that 'the superior character of truth and seriousness in the matter and substance of the best poetry, is inseparable from the superiority of diction and movement marking its style and manner'.

However, Harding's formulation of the ideal which he offers in place of the eighteenth-century ideal of writing ('finding one fully accurate and adequate expression of all that lurks within the

thought') retains a reference to an 'idea' ('the thought') which precedes 'expression' and which the speaker or writer is attempting to
'put into words' as accurately and adequately as possible. I do not
think that this sufficiently allows for transformations of the
'thought' which may occur in the process of composition and (less
frequently perhaps) in the course of conversation. All too often
poems and novels 'take directions' very different from those which
the writer initially 'thought' (or intended) them to take.

I feel sure that Harding would reply that his reference is to '*all
that lurks within* the thought' and that this allows for the possibility
that a poet's (or a speaker's) 'initial thoughts' might undergo
radical transformation as he explores all that lurks within them.

Even then I am still concerned that the analogy or parallel
between those 'common experiences' of 'trying to phrase a complex
state of mind' and the activity of the poet or novelist may be misleading. When, in conversation, we narrate 'an experience' of the
kind I referred to earlier (an incident at work or school, an
encounter with an old friend, a film we have just seen – when these
provoke a 'complex state of mind') there *is* a reality we are trying to
report. And while the phrasing we adopt may, as Harding argues,
approximate to aspects of our state of mind of which we were only
partly, if at all, aware, there remains a reality which we are trying
to express, communicate, put into words. This reference back to a
reality constrains the extent to which our imagination plays 'freely'
with the experience or the thoughts. When we say, 'No, that isn't
quite what I mean,' in circumstances of the kind I have mentioned,
we are not *just* attending to 'some other non-verbal aspects of the
discriminations and attitudes which are emerging', we are 'trying
to get it right' in the sense that we are trying accurately to recount
an actual experience and the (more or less) complex state of mind
to which it gave rise. Some kind of fidelity to what took place and
to what one actually thought and felt remains a primary concern.
To embellish and embroider as does Isadora in *Fear of Flying* is
usually to be untruthful or insincere in real life.

Now I do not think that the poet or the novelist is constrained
in these ways. As T. S. Eliot points out,

We have to communicate – if it is communication, for the word may beg
the question – an experience which is not an experience in the ordinary
sense, *for it may only exist,* formed out of many personal experiences
ordered in some way which may be very different from the way of valua-

tion of practical life, *in the expression of it*. If poetry is a form of 'communication', yet that which is to be communicated is the poem itself and only incidentally the experience and thought which have gone into it. The poem's existence is somewhere between the writer and the reader; it has a reality which is not simply the reality of what the writer is trying to 'express' or of his experience in writing it or of the experience of the reader or of the writer as reader. Consequently the problem of what a poem 'means' is a good deal more difficult than at first appears.[33]

Eliot's comments lead me to be very wary of certain ways of referring to works of literature in terms of their sincerity or insincerity, their 'truth to experience' or the lack of it. Ultimately we have to rely on the convincingness of the words on the page. If they 'make something real' it is often pointless to wonder further about its possible correspondence to the author's experiences or thoughts.

I am moving perilously close to the awkward questions concerning the relevance of an author's intentions and the importance these might have in reading works of literature. While I want to defer this discussion until chapter 7 there is a point about children's writing which I think is worth a mention in the present context. Very often children in school are asked (in various ways) to put their experience into words in an essay, a story or a poem. Very often their work is appraised by the teacher in terms of its sincerity, honesty, or 'truth to experience' (though of course such appraisals may not be communicated to the child). And yet I think there is fundamental uncertainty about what these terms amount to.[34]

I have argued that there are clear connections between the 'truthfulness', 'sincerity' and 'integrity' of literary works and the writing and speaking of everyone, including, of course, children. This argument is intended as a corrective to the mythologizing which often occurs about 'creative writers', which sets them apart, as intimates of the muse, from the rest of ordinary humanity. Now it is often observed that young children's writing has a freshness, a kind of honesty which is often lacking in the work of older children and adults. This must to some extent be due to the fact that the clichés, the conventional phrases, the common currency of adult conversation and writing are less available to the young child who is less liable to be tempted towards distortion or to skid into approximations since he does not possess such a fund of ready-made phrases and conventions. A difficulty for the adult writer or speaker is to get beneath the currency once it is acquired (for who can avoid acquiring it?).

But it must not be assumed (as do the authors of many 'English Method' text-books) that the reality, sincerity or 'truth to experience' to be found in the writing of children (or adults) is – or should be – the product of their *actual* experiences. When children confess apparently deep fears and longings or narrate apparently personal experiences of a particularly vivid kind, the feelings and experiences they 'make real' may only exist *in the expression of them*, formed, perhaps, *out of* many personal experiences, ordered in some way which may be 'very different from the way of valuation of practical life'. In the course of composing a story or a poem the 'communication of experience' may not, in this way, be of 'an experience in the ordinary sense'. Thoughts, feelings and experiences of a 'first-hand' kind mingle with others that they have imagined or read about or heard others express, and become, as it were, 'raw materials' which may be drawn on in *making* something real in the *constructed* 'world' of a poem or story. It is to mislead children (and to fail to appreciate their work) to convey the assumption that the reality or truthfulness of their compositions or poems is dependent upon their recording or reporting their 'actual' feelings and experiences.

What matters, then, in the writing of adults and children, is whether or not the words on the page *make* something real, not whether they are actual *records* of personal experience. Abandoning this criterion of 'reality' and 'truth' in literature puts great pressure on what is 'realization' and how it may be recognized in a work of literature, whether it is written by children or by adults. To attempt to deal with these issues necessitates, of course, an examination of the nature and function of literary criticism. .

2

Literary criticism and literary education

(a) The irreducibility of literature

Any attempt to suggest that literary criticism should form an important part of literary education in schools is met by strong resistance from teachers, aestheticians and philosophers of education. Critical discussion of the kind conducted in universities is thought to be inappropriate in schools largely because it is said to interfere with the immediate pleasure of reading and thus with the development of a wide acquaintance with literature and a taste for reading it. Whether or not this is so is, however, an empirical matter and, so far as I know, there is no research evidence to support the position. If students are 'put off' reading by critical discussion, or if it leads to a cold and clinical approach to literature, this may be due to the inadequacy of the teaching. Teachers who are themselves uncertain of the point of 'critical analysis', except as a means of getting through English exams, are unlikely to generate much sense of its importance and interest to their students.

I have already declared that one of the main contentions of this book is that literary criticism is that form of discourse which undertakes the analysis of works of literature so as to do justice to their 'embodiment' of meaning. I have yet to demonstrate this adequately, but if the importance of this became widely accepted by English teachers then means would undoubtedly be found to ensure that instead of being 'put off' reading literature by critical analysis, their students' interest in literature would be thereby deepened and extended.

Alongside the 'methodological' objections to literary criticism in schools there are also objections of a kind which could broadly be called 'logical' objections. As I will argue in a moment, philosophers of education and aestheticians reject my view that literary criticism is that form of discourse which undertakes the analysis of works of literature so as to do justice to their 'embodiment' of meaning. They maintain that works of literature are 'irreducible' to anything that could be said about them and that, consequently, literary criticism is of little significance in schools. Since criticism cannot, on this view, aspire to be more than external talk 'about' literature of a psychological, historical, sociological or descriptive kind, it is the specialists' concern rather than part of general education in schools.

My dispute with this position is not one which could be settled by empirical research. It depends upon one's conception of the nature of literary critical discourse and its relation to literary works. Some resolution has to be achieved *prior* to any consideration of teaching methods. If I am unable to demonstrate that criticism can do the job I have claimed for it, then it would be pointless to work out the best ways of introducing it to students.

I have carefully separated the 'methodological' from the 'logical' arguments against literary criticism in schools because nearly all my opponents slip from one form of argument to the other. In order to disguise the absence of empirical research to support the methodological argument they make a shift to arguments concerning the 'irreducibility' of works of literature. When this 'logical' analysis runs out of steam, empirical guesswork about the unfortunate effects of teaching literary criticism is offered as if it were incontrovertibly true.

When works of literature variously 'embody', 'enact', 'realize', 'present' their meaning in only 'these words in these positions' there is a sense in which any comment must necessarily be inadequate. I have already argued, for example, that any attempt to paraphrase such a work of literature must fail to do justice to the work in the sense that it cannot accurately reflect its 'organic' interaction of 'form' and 'content'. Unfortunately, however, this vital point has been taken by aestheticians and philosophers of education to imply that such works of literature are inaccessible to interpretation or analysis. Professor L. A. Reid, for example, maintains that when meanings are 'embodied' in works of art, when 'form' and 'content' are inseparable, the 'discursive' or propositional language of criticism is unable to do justice to this 'organic' wholeness. According to Reid, 'the only adequate language of the elucidation of art is the language of art itself'.[1] This belief has gained such a

strong hold that Professor Hirst does not even find it necessary to
elaborate the position and simply takes it as 'readily defensible' that
what is expressed in art can be expressed in no other way and that
art works, including works of literature, are 'irreducible to statements of other kinds'.[2] On this view, literary criticism can offer
only 'knowledge about' literature of an 'external' kind (such as psychological and biographical knowledge about the author or sociological and historical knowledge concerning works of literature).
Literary education is held to be a matter of exposure to works of
literature. 'True' aesthetic knowledge and understanding is a
direct, unanalysed acquaintance with a work of art (Reid);[3] understanding 'the artistic knowledge that works of art themselves state'
which is incommunicable in criticism (Hirst);[4] the product of non-
critical and disinterested attention to a work of art (Stolnitz).[5] John
White exemplifies the aversion to criticism which is a corollary of
advocating a direct unanalysed acquaintance with works of literature : 'when literature's turn does come, instead of reading plenty
of novels and plays to extend their awareness pupils too often have
to change into the slow gear of literary criticism and learn the skills
of a new expertise'.[6] It has to be admitted that all too often literary
criticism is offered as a kind of technical expertise which takes
works of literature as the 'raw material' for a form of highly
mechanized processing in the academic factories. However, it is just
as mistaken to dismiss the connection between the development of
awareness through literature and the activity of literary criticism.
If we were to estimate the value of any discipline on the evidence
of its worst educational practice there would be a mass exodus from
universities and schools to the beaches and the pubs. The fact is,
however, that some critics reject White's view of literary criticism :

> To insist on this critical work as discipline is not to contemplate the
> elaboration of technical apparatus and drill. . . Such help as can be given
> the student will not be in the nature of initiation into technical pro-
> cedures and there is no apparatus to be handed over – a show of such in
> analytic work will most likely turn out to be a substitute for the use
> of intelligence upon the text.[7]

Remarks such as these indicate F. R. Leavis' concern to avoid any
characterization of criticism which could lead it to be viewed as a
'rigid technique' and consequently as an irrelevant and mechanical
distraction from reading literary works. Leavis has done more than
anyone else to promote the importance of literary criticism as a

'discipline' in literary education. But he attentively maintains a high degree of flexibility in his use of critical concepts. He opposes any attempt to rigidify such notions as 'thought' or 'imagery' or 'movement' in literature or to draw sharp boundaries between such concepts. He is aware that this would lead to critical strait-jacketing of poems instead of the 'mirroring' of the relations between aspects of a poem which criticism at best makes possible.

These comments anticipate the account of literary criticism which I will offer in the next section. The point I want to make here is that Leavis does not see the difficulty of articulating a response to the elusive qualities of literature as a reason for abandoning criticism and getting students simply to 'love' poetry or merely to 'contemplate' it. Instead he develops a mode of discourse which attempts to do justice to the organic quality, the 'wholeness' of works of literature. Many literary critics are just as aware as are the educational theorists of the dangers of 'murdering to dissect'. But Bradley's reminder, for example, that 'in true poetry it is, in strictness, impossible to express the meaning in any but its own words, or to change the words without changing the meaning' does not deter him from attempting to write criticism which does justice to the unparaphrasable qualities of 'true poetry'.[8]

Sonia Greger is rare among those educational theorists and aestheticians who emphasize the irreducibility of literature and the consequent inadequacy of criticism because she actually comments on a work of literature in order to support her position. In the light of an analysis of Blake's 'The Sick Rose' she says :

So many possible or potential meanings, held at the threshold of consciousness, are controlled by the words of the poem and held in suspension so that the reader has a disturbing 'feeling of significance' which eludes discursive analysis. The only way in which all the potential meanings can be expressed in precisely this relationship is in the words of the poem itself. We can talk *about* different aspects of the poem – analyse them – but to experience Blake's particular synthesis we must read or listen to Blake's poem. This is what Reid means by 'meaning-embodied'.[9]

The only part of this which might lead us to doubt the adequacy of criticism is that dimension of the poem which Greger says eludes discursive analysis. Of course it is only those words of the poem in those relationships which precisely express all the potential meanings it contains and of course there is no *other* way of 'experiencing Blake's poem'. But it is absurd to expect a critical analysis to give rise to the experience of the poem or to precisely express all the potential meanings in a work of literature. Critical analysis is not concerned to *replace* works of literature and such a test for the adequacy of criticism is misconceived. All criticism can claim to do is to elucidate aspects of a work of literature in ways which respect the relations between the aspects and the whole. With some works of literature it may be peculiarly difficult to comment with any adequacy on the elusive sources of our response. But to emphasize this is to ignore the very great range of literary works when the critic *can* comment with a high degree of appropriateness and insight on qualities and significances he has perceived. The elusive qualities are a special kind of challenge because they stretch the adequacy of the critical comment. Consider T. S. Eliot's comment on Marvell's poem 'Nymph and Faun' : 'Marvell takes a slight affair, the feeling of a girl for her pet, and gives it a connexion with that inexhaustible and terrible nebula of emotion that surrounds all our exact and practical passions and mingles with them.'[10] Eliot registers the mysterious depth of the poem and identifies a quality of our 'felt aesthetic experience', an experience with the kind of 'immediacy' upon which the opponents of criticism place so much emphasis. And while Eliot's point about the poem could be developed further by the critic it need not follow that the elusiveness of the poem would thus be dispelled. In poetry such as Blake's and Marvell's a kind of elusiveness is frequently present. To respond to and register the elusiveness of the connections in their poetry is often to 'fully understand' this aspect of what they create. (There is no need to invoke some 'meaning' that 'lies always beyond our grasp'.)

Sonia Greger joins the aestheticians and philosophers of education who reject the significance of criticism in literary education by insisting on the overriding significance of that which is inexpressible or difficult to articulate about a work of literature. This is puzzling because her detailed analysis of 'The Sick Rose' goes a long way towards doing justice to its embodied meaning and also because her educational programme sees dialogue between student and teacher as the most important part.

It is not a case of one person 'interpreting' the meaning of a work but being unable to express anything at all of this meaning, so that the non-aesthetic person remains forever in the company of the philistines. On the contrary I believe that everyone *can* experience aesthetically and would have much to offer in dialogue about art and natural beauty, but that many have had this capacity rendered sterile by an upbringing and education which lays all stress upon analytical reason.[11]

When she refers here to the 'aesthetic experience' which she believes everyone could have, Greger no longer seems to mean that this is an experience which 'eludes discursive analysis'. Dialogue is possible about it, though apparently it is to be conducted without employing analytical reasoning. It is far from clear what particular form of reasoning is being opposed here. Is the reasoning of critics such as Bradley, Eliot and Leavis 'analytic' and thus to be rejected? When Leavis analyses the nature of the imagery in Blake's 'The Sick Rose' in order to demonstrate the way in which imagery need not be visual,[12] he helps us to see how the (non-discursive) poem works, although his own argument is, of course, discursive. Such critics 'reason' about works of literature and 'analyse' them. They employ analytical reasoning characteristic of literary criticism and it would be quite inappropriate for them to apply the terms and criteria of analysis of a philosopher, for example. Pointing out the contradictions in Donne's poetry would be a manifestly futile endeavour (unless this led on to an exploration of the significance of the contradictions). It is difficult to know what the opponents of criticism are dismissing when they dismiss 'logical' or 'analytical' reasoning about works of art, but in so far as they are dismissing literary criticism in general they exhibit a misconception of the nature and function of critical argument.

I have emphasized that crude paraphrases of the 'thought' of a work of literature of the sort which bad teachers expect of their unfortunate students at exam time are worse than useless. We may safely assume that Sonia Greger would regard her own account of Blake's poem as getting closer to identifying 'Blake's particular synthesis' than such exercises are likely to achieve. The point is that 'discursive literary critical analysis' is an attempt to convey the critic's experience of the (often elusive) qualities of a poem, an attempt which may be more or less successful.

Consider, for example, Leavis' comments on the function of the words 'deep and broad' in this passage from *Macbeth*:

> All our service
> In every point twice done, and then done double,
> Were poor and single business to contend
> Against those honours deep and broad wherewith
> Your majesty loads our house.
>
> (Act I, Scene vi)

This may seem to be just a rather elaborate way of saying, 'I'm very pleased you came.' Or, if it is an exhaustive account of the meaning that is required, would this do?

Even if our services to you could have been quadrupled they would have amounted to very little in comparison with the honour you do us by staying in our house.

When Leavis analyses the passage he points out that if we attend to the interactions of all the words then the key words in the creation of meaning here are those which at first seem to be merely decorative. The words are 'deep and broad', which the paraphrase simply ignored as being inessential to the meaning. Leavis observes that 'those adjectives describe a river, and whether we tell ourselves so or not, the presence of a river makes itself felt in the effect of the passage',[13] and he goes on to show how the adjectives, in their unique conjunction with 'honours', transform and make real the meaning. Leavis leaves implicit the importance these subtleties have in relation to the rest of the play and these could be made clear. Macbeth is to kill the King – this is the overtone of 'contend'. But by doing so, Macbeth is to cut himself off from the fount of honour (the King). It is impossible, however, to contend success-fully against a river 'deep and broad' – and Macbeth is to be destroyed, physically and spiritually, as a result of his attempt. The King's honours are indeed a 'load' for Macbeth and the critic would analyse the meaning of 'load' largely in terms of such reverberations – such suggestions are part of its meaning.

Leavis is discussing an 'elusive' quality in the passage – as he says, the presence of a river 'makes itself felt' in the effect of the passage, 'whether we tell ourselves so or not'. We don't have to be able to articulate (as the critic does) how the words 'deep and broad' function in the passage to have an awareness of their func-tioning. The absence of explicitness in the metaphor leaves the meaning 'at the threshold of consciousness' (as Greger puts it about Blake's poem) and there it will remain for most readers. There is nothing peculiar about this. Every day, in our interaction with other people, we are responding to elusive aspects of their com-munication with us. In chapter 1 (section (c)) I pointed out that unparaphrasable and subtle features of our non-verbal experience are often captured in tone of voice, facial expression, gesture, hesitation, etc. which interact with our words in ways which are analogous to the way in which the words of a literary work subtly interact with rhythm, tone, juxtaposition, stress, etc. Much of the time we may not be able to say exactly what it was that led us to take up what someone says in the way we do and most of the time we don't need to scrutinize subtleties of this sort. Much of the time in reading works of literature we don't need to analyse the elusive significances which 'make themselves felt'. But they are, in general, analysable, and we may be asked to justify our response to a poem just as we may be asked to explain why we responded to someone's remarks as we did. Our success in justifying our response to a poem will depend on how capable a critic we are.

My argument in this section has been that philosophers of education and aestheticians have misunderstood what is implied by referring to the 'uniqueness', 'untranslatability', 'irreducibility' or the 'autonomy' of works of literature. All these terms refer to an important characteristic of (good) works of literature, that 'what' they say is inseparably part of the 'way' they say it. With such a conception as Matthew Arnold's of the connection between form and content in 'the best poetry' (see p. 17 above) the critic will not be tempted to tear the 'thought' out of the delicate organic structure of a work of literature. It is a mistake to assume that the embodied nature of art structures, the intricate unity of a work of art, are inaccessible to critical analysis conducted in a language which does justice to the ultimate irreducibility of works of art but engages with them fully. Coleridge's famous description of the poet's activity may be seen to imply an activity on the part of the reader which in some sense corresponds with that of the poet. 'The poet, described in ideal perfection, brings the whole soul of man into activity.'[14] The critic, described in ideal perfection, is one who can elucidate and, hopefully, prompt in others the activity that the poem promotes. Such criticism is not itself 'the language of art', of course. But neither is it merely talk 'about' art of an external kind. It is a mode of discourse finely tuned to the characterization, analysis and judgement of works of art, as I will attempt to illustrate in a moment.

There is no mysterious realm of purely aesthetic knowledge somehow inaccessibly buried in the unanalysable organic intricacy of works of art. If a critic is to do justice to the organic quality of works of art then he will require a highly agile and flexible mode of discourse to articulate it. We may be wary of introducing our students to such a mode of discourse prior to a wide acquaintance with works of literature since there are dangers of developing a facile slickness which skates over the surface of a work or strait-jackets it in technicalities. In certain circumstances (with particular children in particular schools) we may find we can do little more in the time available than promote a wide acquaintance with works of literature or a favourable disposition towards literature. But methodological points about the best way of teaching something are largely contingent or circumstantial and are not to be confused with logical points about what constitutes knowledge, understanding or judgement in this or any other domain.[15]

(b) **Testing literary appreciation**

I have pointed out that misconceptions of the sense in which literary works are 'irreducible' to what we might say about them lead to the mistaken belief that our apprehension of a work of literature is incapable of articulation. It has even been claimed that this incommunicable intuition of meaning in literature and art is available only to those with special faculties or qualifications. According to Reid, it is

Only by being an artist or by possessing aesthetic sensibility, can I make, or know, the embodiment which is art. A category may be in our minds or at the back of our minds but we have to make from these the 'aesthetic leap'. If (in some conscious philosophical mood) I recognize this piece of art as a piece of embodiment, I can only do so by first exercising an act of aesthetic intuition, which, as I have repeatedly said, is a *sui generis* form of indwelling knowledge. . . Talk of a category like embodiment can only be understood by someone who is not only a philosopher, but who already knows art from the inside. It means nothing to a philistine or to an artistically raw person.[16]

Since schoolrooms tend to contain a pretty high proportion of philistines and artistically raw people the outlook for literary education looks bleak. Works of art can only be understood by certain sorts of people – those with 'aesthetic sensibility', 'aesthetic intuition' who are capable of 'aesthetic leaps'. If an 'artistically raw person' were to claim that a poem was embodied and offered an analysis of the way form and content in a poem interact organically, we could not, on these grounds, assume that he really did appreciate, understand or 'know' the poem. What we would need to find out is whether or not he has exercised an act of aesthetic intuition. But since this is a *sui generis* form of indwelling knowledge, how are we to determine this? Perhaps Reid would say that someone who gave a critical account which showed an acute awareness of the way a poem embodied its meaning could not, for this very reason, be an 'artistically raw person'. But if this were so, to speak of artistic rawness, lack of sensibility, failure to make aesthetic leaps or exercise acts of aesthetic intuition is to say no more than that there is no evidence in what the person says critically about poems that shows perception of their aesthetic quality.

Both Reid and Hirst fail to see that someone's 'appreciation' of a literary work, his 'knowledge' of it, his perception of its 'truth' (and this applies to the several senses which Hirst and Reid attach to these terms) can only be evidenced in the remarks he makes about it. It is in this sense that criticism is an articulation of our apprehension or appreciation of art.[17] We may hypothesize as we wish about the psychological states, the leaps and exercises and feelings that he underwent in order to arrive at his perceptions but such hypotheses cannot form the basis for a judgement that x recognizes, understands, appreciates or knows a work of literature or art.

The prevailing distrust of criticism in philosophy of education finds its most extreme statement in Diane Collinson's paper on 'Aesthetic education' which is given unfortunate prominence by being collected in *New Essays in the Philosophy of Education*.[18] Mental athletics of the sort which Reid favours are complemented by more overt physical performances as indications of a person's aesthetic involvement and aesthetic education. Criticism (referred to as 'fluent aesthetic commentating') is seen to be quite distinct from aesthetic involvement or aesthetic education. Instead of attending to the remarks someone makes about works of art in order to determine whether he is aesthetically involved or aesthetically educated we should, according to Collinson, be attending to such features of his overt behaviour as a 'stance of inertia' or 'rapt attention' before a painting. For the aesthetically involved person these may be succeeded by 'stepping back from the work', 'moving closer or to one side of it', placing the painting in a different light or at a different level, 'turning away from it and then wheeling around to see it suddenly and afresh from a new angle'.[19] Collinson sees 'little room in this activity for what I have called aesthetic commentating'.

But this is quite misleading. It is entirely an empirical matter whether or not aesthetically educated people act in these ways –

the connection between such activities and aesthetic involvement and aesthetic education is entirely contingent. Whereas if the comments that someone offers on a work of art entirely misconceive the work then it doesn't matter a jot how he stands or walks nor does it matter whether he is 'involved'. There is a necessary connection between perceiving works of art appropriately and being aesthetically involved and aesthetically educated. If you can't perceive them appropriately then you can't respond to them appropriately. The only test we have of this is in what people say critically about works of art.

Of course it is of the utmost importance to insist that what people say about works of literature and art may not be *sufficient* as a test of aesthetic involvement or of aesthetic education. I have already acknowledged that when literature and art appreciation become examinable 'subjects' there is often a tendency to counterfeit responses to works of art or even simply to copy or ape the accounts which are offered by teachers and text-books. This is certainly a danger but it is one which must be seen as part of a general educational problem rather than as one which is peculiar to the testing of literary understanding, appreciation and discrimination. The conditions of competitive mass schooling (which are so often inimical to education[20]) are such that students are often encouraged to take short cuts and to offer second-hand, half-grasped judgements provided by teachers and text-books. This is frequently true of university 'education' as well. Rarely do examinations probe the understanding – they encourage a superficial imitation of judgement and argument in every subject with which I am familiar. Perhaps the regurgitation of teacher and text-book material is more objectionable when works of literature are concerned than the regurgitation, without understanding, of teacher and text-book material in history and geography, but I have never seen this argued. Unless this can be established, the problem of copying, without understanding, cannot be said to be peculiar to the teaching and testing of literary understanding and appreciation and ought not to lead us to abandon criticism in literary education any more than it should lead us to abandon historical, social or economic analysis and dialogue in education. Rather, it should constitute a challenge to the adequacy of our teaching in all these domains.

I do not think we can take literally Leavis' claim that 'an

approach [to works of literature] is personal or it is nothing : you
cannot take over the appreciation of a poem, and unappreciated,
the poem isn't "there".' There is an obvious sense in which we can
'take over' the appreciation of a poem – it is in this sense that we
could come to agree with some of Leavis' own appreciations.[21] To
this, no doubt, Leavis would reply that if we have not checked his
accounts with the literature he discusses and found them to be
more satisfactory than our own readings then we are not appreciating the works in question but just counterfeiting his own. I have
acknowledged that this is a danger when criticism is introduced
in schools and universities. It is tempting when confronted with
large numbers of students to invite them to 'take over' one's own
analysis in this way, however we might disguise it by question and
answer techniques, however much we provide the illusion of collaboration. And this can result in 'appreciations' being offered
which are next to 'nothing' because not personal. On the other
hand it is possible that better (more attentive, more open) readers
than ourselves will offer us an analysis which we do want to 'take
over' and make our own.

It is a tempting fallacy, as well, to think that an untutored
response will necessarily be more honest, more personal than a
tutored response. Children (and adults) often bring all kinds of
prejudices, irrelevant assumptions and stock responses to the reading of literature. They have often been 'taught' to dislike anything
in verse, even, perhaps, anything in words rather than in pictures.
It takes very tactful teaching, over a considerable period of time, to
shift such prejudices and develop a responsive disposition towards
literature. At a more sophisticated level the prejudices and misconceptions often stem from teaching which has encouraged
students to treat works of literature as elaborate ways of saying
something which could be put more simply or directly in other
words, i.e. from teaching which misconceives or ignores the crucial
interaction of form and content in literature. I have argued that
the 'thought' of literary works cannot be separated from the other
aspects with which it is in interaction – imagery, movement, feeling, etc. Learning to respond adequately to literary works and
learning to articulate this response is, in part, learning to employ a
form of discourse which can do justice to this organic interaction.
In what follows I will be more specific about the nature of such
criticism.

(c) The relations between literary critical concepts

The most fundamental challenge to the literary critic is one which should be of great concern to the literature teacher – how to talk about *aspects* of works of literature without implying that the aspects are separable from the whole. How often, in classrooms, are students invited to sub-divide their account of the novel they have been reading under headings such as 'characterization', 'description', 'dialogue', 'incident', 'theme', etc.? If the novel is, as Lawrence claimed, 'the highest example of subtle interrelatedness that man has discovered', how likely is it that the students will perceive this interrelatedness if their energies are devoted to dissection and dismembering?

In *The Art of Fiction*, in 1884, Henry James discusses the relationship between 'characterization', 'description', 'dialogue' and 'incident' in the novel.

People often talk of these things as if they had a kind of internecine distinctness, instead of melting into one another at every breath, and being intimately associated parts of one general effort of expression. I cannot imagine composition existing in a series of blocks, nor conceive, in any novel worth discussing at all, of a passage of description that is not in its intention narrative, a passage of dialogue that is not in its intention descriptive, a touch of truth of any sort that does not partake of the nature of incident or an incident that derives its interest from any other source than the general and only source of the success of a work of art – that of being illustrative.[22] A novel is a living thing, all one and continuous, like any other organism, and in proportion as it lives will it be found that in each of the parts there is something of each of the other parts. The critic who over the close texture of a finished work shall pretend to trace a geography of items will mark some frontiers as artificial, I fear, as any that have been known to history.[23]

In the previous chapter I discussed a passage from Pope's *Dunciad* which dramatizes or 'enacts' the point that in literature, 'parts relate to parts [and] they to whole', and Pope, too, uses the analogy of an 'organism'. I pointed out how crucial in this enactment was a single semi-colon, and James insists that in 'successful stories', as well, 'every word and every punctuation point contribute directly to the expression'. The passage in which he says this is worth citing partly because it bears a strong resemblance to Matthew Arnold's account (written four years earlier, in 1880) of the relationship between form and content in 'the best poetry' (see above, p. 17):

in proportion as the work is successful the idea permeates and penetrates it, informs and animates it, so that every word and punctuation point contribute directly to the expression, in that proportion do we lose our sense of the story being a blade which may be drawn more or less out of its sheath. The story and the novel, the idea and the form, are the needle and thread, and I never heard of a guild of tailors who recommended the use of the thread without the needle or the needle without the thread.[24]

I offered a minor illustration of James' point in my earlier comments on Erica Jong's novel *Fear of Flying*. The success of the passage I cited from the novel (on the first page of the previous chapter) depends upon a delicate control of tone which reflects from sentence to sentence the shifting currents in Isadora's consciousness, currents which dramatize the uncertainties about 'truth' in life and 'truth' in literature with which the novel is concerned. The reader is subtly drawn into Isadora's facile and self-deceptive meanderings about literature and life just as he is drawn into a prurient, even voyeuristic, interest in Isadora's sexual exploits. And when Erica Jong exposes or plays with our credulity, we are made aware of some of our own uncertainties and self-deceptions about 'truth' in life and in literature. 'What' the novel is 'about' in such passages is not separable from the details of its manner or 'style' of narration. In proportion as *Fear of Flying* is successful its 'ideas' 'permeate and penetrate it, inform and animate it', so that every syntactical shift (and the 'punctuation points' that determine these) contribute directly to the expression. In so far as the novel fails, its expression ceases to be animated by its ideas and the ideas are not brought to life by the expression.[25]

Arnold Kettle's discussion of *Oliver Twist*, in his *Introduction to the English Novel*, is of interest here because he draws attention to the way one of the 'elements' in this novel, the plot, *fails* to partake of the other elements and thus constitutes a deep flaw in the book. 'The centre of interest, the essential pattern in the novel, is not its plot, and it is the major fault of the plot that it does not correspond with this central interest.' In Kettle's view,

The core of the novel, and what gives it value is its consideration of the plight of the poor. Its pattern is the contrasted relation of two worlds – the underworld of the workhouse, the funeral, the thieves' kitchen and the comfortable world of the Brownlows and Mailies. It is this pattern that stamps the novel on our minds. We do not remember, when we think back on it, the intricacies of the plot; we are not interested in the affairs of Rose and Harry Mailie; we do not care who Oliver's father was and, though we sympathize with Oliver's struggles, we do not mind whether or not he gets his fortune. What we do remember is that vision of the underworld of the first eleven chapters, the horror of Fagin, the fate of Mr Bumble, the trial of the Artful Dodger, the murder of Nancy, the end of Sikes. What engages our sympathy is not Oliver's feeling for the mother he never saw, but his struggle against his oppressors of which the famous gruel scene is indeed a central and adequate symbol.

The contrast of the two worlds is at the very heart of the novel, so that we see a total picture of contrasted darkness and light. . . The plot makes impossible the realization of the living pattern and conflict of the book.[26]

Kettle points out how the 'silly and mechanical' plot of *Oliver Twist* is inseparable from ('partakes of') the 'characterization' in the novel. In so far as Oliver is part of the 'living pattern and conflict of the book' he becomes 'a figure of symbolic significance'.

Because he is *all* workhouse orphans the lack of a convincing individual psychology does not matter; it is Oliver's situation rather than himself that moves us and the situation is presented with all of Dickens' dramatic symbolic power.[27]

However, once Oliver becomes involved in the plot, his entire symbolic significance changes.

Until he wakes up in Mr Brownlow's house he is a poor boy struggling against the inhumanity of the state. After he has slept himself into the Brownlow world he is a young bourgeois who has been done out of his property.[28]

In the opening chapters of the book, 'poverty is revealed in a light which makes the facile terms of good and bad irrelevant', but by the end of the book, 'Nancy can be pigeon-holed as good, Sikes as bad. But who can say whether the starving creatures of the opening chapters are good or bad?' The failure of the plot 'partakes of' the failure of the characterization and the plot 'expresses an interpretation of life infinitely less profound and honest than the novel itself reveals'. In Henry James' terminology the 'idea' of *Oliver Twist* does not 'permeate and penetrate' the plot, does not 'inform and animate it'.

The inseparability of 'style' of narration in fiction from other 'elements' such as 'characterization' is often so unobtrusive in the work of a novelist such as Jane Austen that we simply take it for granted. A rather striking illustration of the way 'style' and 'character' 'partake' of one another is, nevertheless, provided in the contrast between the first and second volumes of *Persuasion*. Several critics have pointed out that, in volume one, Anne Elliot is presented as the commanding centre, partly because the narrative is 'slanted' through her. 'Narrative, authorial comment, dialogue and interior monologue merge into one another'[29] and 'free indirect speech', in which lengthy dialogue is compressed and located within the central consciousness, gives the sense that the novel takes place within the mind of the heroine. In a recent collection of essays Walton Litz points out the changes that occur in volume two.

But this complex method of internalized presentation is most evident in the first volume, and in volume 2 – as Anne Elliot enters the alien world of Bath – Jane Austen reverts to . . . more objective methods. It is a sign of Anne's isolation that the revelation of William Elliot's true nature, and even of Wentworth's love, must come to her through letters, one of the most 'external' of fictional devices.[30]

There is some inappropriateness here in referring to Jane Austen's mode of narration as a 'device'.[31] Litz's point is that the 'externality' or 'objectivity' of the 'style' of narration is integral to Anne's 'characterization' and to the way in which the reader perceives her isolation. The 'formal elements' are not separable 'means' by which 'content' is presented. The mode of narration is constitutive of 'what' is created, it dramatizes Anne's isolation.

In the same collection of essays, Malcolm Bradbury argues against the widely accepted view that the 'action' of *Persuasion* appears as 'a collection of chance incidents stretching out until all the various mechanical confusions have been put right, and the predictable can happen'. An important strand in Bradbury's rejection of this account is that the 'events' are significant in terms of the development of Anne Elliot's character.

Anne's development in the novel is more substantial than most critics allow. She accepts as a given standard of her social world the dangers of lowering herself, and it is necessary that we realize this if the persuasion of Lady Russell is to seem to us rightly accepted by her. It is the subsequent events which show Lady Russell wrong, not the grounds on which she persuaded Anne; Anne comes to an understanding more radical than even a good woman like her can conceive of.[32] If those events do have any order and meaning for a novelist with the controlling exactness that we know Jane Austen to have had, then surely their pattern takes its order from her development in her understanding of her situation.[33]

The details of Bradbury's case are not essential to the point I am concerned with, which is about the presuppositions of the argument between Bradbury and his opponents. According to the latter, *Persuasion* is unsuccessful because the action, the pattern of events in the novel seems to them to be largely separable from character development. Bradbury's case is that, on the contrary, Anne's development as a character depends upon her understanding of the significance of the events – it is this that gives them 'order and meaning'. Bradbury thus meets the charge that *Persuasion* is fragmented, that its 'parts' do not cohere and 'partake' of one another and argues for the novel's successful integration of 'character' and 'event' as part of an animating pattern in the novel.

Each of the examples I have selected reveals the critics' attempt to demonstrate, in relation to the novels they discuss, 'how parts relate to parts and they to whole'. The very existence of a critical vocabulary, with terms such as 'plot', 'characterization', 'dialogue', etc., entails the inevitability of some degree of compartmentalization and fragmentation when we discuss works of fiction. A crucial measure of the success of criticism is the extent to which the critic can employ such concepts in ways which minimize the dismembering and fragmentation of literary works and the extent to which the critic can reveal that 'in proportion as [a novel] lives will it be found that in each of the parts there is something of each of the other parts'.

I would like to think that the point that my examples are designed to illustrate is one that is too obvious to warrant such emphasis and expansion. But I know from my own experience how tempting it is to employ a simplified and compartmentalized critical vocabulary in teaching. And I do not underestimate the difficulty, the challenge, of introducing students to ways of discussing novels in which the interpenetration of the 'elements' in the novels is reflected in the 'overlapping' of critical concepts. Both teachers and students have a natural preference for employing terms in readily definable and categorical ways – it's easier to *learn* these and thus easier to teach them. But since 'elements' of successful novels do not *exist* independently of one another, the critical concepts that refer to these 'elements' must reflect a high degree of interdependence as well.

It may well be that this fundamental challenge to the literary critic and to the literature teacher is best approached through poetry. The concentration of poetry may manifest in a more graspable compass the 'close texture' to which Henry James refers and make it less likely that the critic or the teacher will 'pretend to trace a geography of items' and 'mark artificial frontiers'.

In recent times the critic whose work most amply demonstrates how critical concepts may be employed to imply the necessary interaction and inseparability of the 'elements' in 'the best poetry' is F. R. Leavis. Leavis' work is also of particular interest in the present context since he was highly attentive to the implications of his work for teaching. Leavis claims that 'the best critical terms and concepts one can find or provide oneself with will always be inadequate to the varied complexities with which the critic has to deal'.[34] Yet I think that he has provided us with a number of critical concepts which are 'adequate' to the particular kind of complexity with which I am concerned. His 'analytic practice' seems to me to be 'valid' in the way he himself demands: 'Valid analytic practice is a strengthening of the sense of relevance: scrutiny of the parts must at the same time be an effort towards fuller realization of the whole and all appropriate play of intelligence . . . is controlled by an implicit concern for a total value judgement.'[35] I will point out that the relations between the key concepts in Leavis' criticism are such as to make it logically impossible for anyone employing the concepts to refer to 'aspects of' or 'elements in' a poem without at the same time referring to the interaction of the 'elements' in the whole work.

The key concepts are those which refer to the 'aspects of' or 'elements in' a poem, e.g. 'imagery', 'movement', 'rhythm', 'thought', 'feeling'. In Leavis' criticism these concepts interpenetrate or 'partake' of one another. 'Imagery', for example, is used to some extent co-extensively with 'movement'. 'Thought', as Leavis employs this concept, has to some extent the same meaning as 'feeling'. Thus if a critic employing these concepts refers to a poem's 'thought' he must necessarily be implying something about the 'feeling' of the poem. If he refers to the 'imagery' he must necessarily be implying something about the 'movement'. The relations are more subtle and complex than this, of course, but some degree of schematization is inevitable to begin with.

It must be made clear, however, that I am not trying to reduce the criticism of Leavis or of anyone else to a rigidly schematized 'technique'. Some philosophers do give the impression that this is not only possible but necessary if criticism is ever to be taken seriously as a discipline.[36] Leavis is rightly concerned that the flexibility of the relations between critical concepts be maintained – any rigidifying of what can be meant by 'thought' or 'imagery' in poetry, for example, or of the relations between such concepts, could lead to critical strait-jacketing of poems instead of the 'mirroring' of the relations between aspects of poems which Leavis' use of critical terminology makes possible. Leavis was always opposed to any attempt to generalize on these matters. When he asks, 'What is metaphor?', 'What is imagery?' he replies : 'I do not think that much profit is likely to come of trying to answer these questions directly in general terms.'[37] As a result he goes to considerable lengths to make it difficult for a commentator to pull out a 'technical apparatus' from his criticism. This is not perversity but an acute awareness of the dangers of facile distortion and dilution of criticism in education. As he said, 'Such help as can be given the student will not be in the nature of initiations into technical procedures.' My intention, then, is not to describe a 'technical apparatus' for the use of students but rather to offer an account of Leavis' use of critical concepts which does justice to their flexibility.

In three essays which were recently re-published Leavis is much more explicit than elsewhere in his criticism about the interrelations between the critical concepts he employs, although he still maintains a close attention to particular poems selected to bring the concepts sharply into play. The titles of the essays set out some of the key concepts with which he is concerned : ' "Thought" and emotional quality', 'Imagery and movement', 'Reality and sincerity'.[38]

Discussing Blake's 'best verse' in the first of these essays, Leavis remarks on its superiority over and its extreme unlikeness to Shelley's poetry :

If we are to associate [Blake's] essential strength with the 'thing seen', it must be in the full consciousness that the phrase here has more than its literal sense. The essential objects in its pre-occupation with which his poetry exhibits such purity of interest – such disinterestedness – are not susceptible of visualisation; they belong to inner experience, emotional and instinctive life, the inner life of the psyche. It is Blake's genius that dealing with material that could be present to him only as the most intimate personal experience – the very substance of his appetites, desires, inner urgencies, fears and temptations – he can write poetry that has virtues analogous to those of the 'wiry bounding line' . . . he demanded of visual art. . . Its intensity is not one of emotional insistence; there is none of the Shelleyan 'I feel, I suffer, I yearn'; there is no atmosphere of feeling and no I. . . . What distinguishes Blake's poetry from Shelley's may fairly be said to be a presence of 'thought'. The 'seeing' elements of our inner experience as clearly defined objects involves, of itself, something we naturally call 'thought'. And it will be noted how inevitably we slip into the visual analogy, the type and model of objectivity being the thing seen (there are bearings here on the visualist fallacy in criticism); and, further, that there is the significant linguistic usage by which to 'see' is to understand ('I see!').[39]

Leavis is here pointing out the way Blake's poetry, which is frequently vividly visual (in an admittedly peculiar way), shows the presence not so much of 'imagery' as of 'thought'. The concept of 'imagery' and the concept of 'thought' in poetry are both extended, and they are extended into each other, as it were. The terms 'partake of one another', they become to some degree co-extensive.

A different but related point about 'imagery' appears in Leavis' comments on Keats' 'Ode to Autumn', a poem in which he says, 'the relation between the firmness of the art and the firm grasp on the outer world appears most plainly'.[40]

> To bend with apples the moss'd cottage trees,
> And fill all fruit with ripeness to the core;
> To swell the gourd and plump the hazel shells
> With a sweet kernel

Leavis comments that the packed consonants in 'moss'd cottage trees' and 'the unpoetical "plump"' in their 'sensuous firmness' introduce 'tactual images' – 'meaning, that is, has from first to last its inseparable and essential part in the effect of the "sound"'. This, in turn, may be dependent on the movement of the lines:

> And sometimes like a gleaner thou dost keep
> Steady thy laden head across a brook.

Leavis points out that 'in the step from the rime-word "keep" across (so to speak) the pause enforced by the line division, to "steady" the balancing movement of the gleaner is enacted'.[41] 'Movement', 'sound', 'imagery' and 'thought' are concepts which, in Leavis' criticism, are thickly interrelated. The movement of the lines or the sound of the words may tactually or physically *image* the meaning ('there may be images that engage any of the senses a poet may appeal to').[42] 'The word "image" itself tends to encourage the notion that imagery is necessarily visual, and the visualistic fallacy is widespread.' But just as we have 'non-visual' imagery in the lines from Keats, so, in Blake, the visual elements show the presence not so much of 'imagery' as of 'thought'.

It is important to note, however, that Leavis is not merely stipulatively redefining terms. The mental process he describes as something we naturally call thought ('seeing elements of our inner experience as clearly defined objects') focuses an area of actual overlap in the application of the terms 'thought' and 'imagery'. Leavis is reminding us that we sometimes think in images, that images may be the medium of thought. And since poetry characteristically employs imagery, the implication is that in good poetry the imagery necessarily partakes of the thought – the thought permeates and animates it, and any frontier that the critic sets up between such aspects will be artificial.

The relationship between 'thought' and 'feeling' in poetry is one that particularly preoccupies Leavis. In ' "Thought" and emotional quality' Leavis compares Lawrence's 'Piano' with Tennyson's 'Tears, Idle Tears'[43] and it is 'movement' that is emphasized at first. The movement of 'Piano' is subtler than the simple plangent flow of Tennyson's poem, and it has a stating manner that controls the dangerous emotional swell. From this Leavis develops his comments on the 'thought' and 'feeling' of 'Piano'. To summarize this development, Leavis sees the stating movement as associated with a 'particularizing' that is 'unbeglamouring', 'which is at the same time in some measure a placing. That is, sensibility in the poem doesn't work in complete divorce from intelligence; feeling is not divorced from thinking; however the key terms are to be defined, these propositions at any rate have a clear enough meaning in their context'. Leavis is turning to the ostensive clarification of terms noted earlier and certainly his full analysis is essential for a complete understanding of the relations he sees existing here between such terms as 'thinking', 'feeling' and 'movement'. But the main relation is identified by the term 'placing'. The nostalgic emotion in the poem is qualified, there is a 'disinterested evaluation' of the nostalgia. This qualification (or 'distancing' or 'placing') of the nostalgia is achieved by the 'un-

beglamouring' presence of the sharply perceived particular situation, the 'tinkly' piano, and the stating movement controlling the
emotional swell. This 'placing' is responsible for the poem's 'poise',
a frequent term of praise in the criticism. In this case it refers to
the balancing of 'the flood of remembrance' against the critical
attitude towards the emotion evoked by the situation. 'Poise' simply
means that a poem has *successfully* 'placed' or balanced its diverse
elements. In the case of 'Piano' the poem is judged to be successful
because 'However strong an emotional effect the poem has, it is
essentially conditioned or placed by "thought"; the constating,
relating and critical mind has its essential part in the work of
sensibility.'[44]

Before any further comment on this I want to juxtapose it with
certain comments Leavis makes on metaphysical poetry. For his
account of the relation between 'thought' and 'feeling' has an
emphasis which is the reverse of that noted above. Metaphysical
'vices', he says, 'are a matter not of the cultivation of emotion for
its own sake, but of the cultivation of subtlety of thought for its own
sake; we find ingenuities of analogy and logic (or quasi-logic) that
are uncontrolled by a total imaginative or emotional purpose'.[45]
The concept of 'thought' interpenetrates that of 'feeling' or 'emotion', just as the notion of 'imagery' was seen to be to some extent
co-extensive with 'thought'. A poem's 'feeling' necessarily enters
into its 'thinking' and vice versa. Leavis views their inseparability
as being so complete that the absence of one is more than a
symptom of the absence of the other – it is almost a test of its
absence. So it is not surprising that we later find Leavis saying of
a poem by Lionel Johnson[46] that the poet 'aims straight at emotion' and 'by-passing thought misses any real substantial emotion'.
Whereas in Marvell's 'Horatian Ode', with which Johnson's poem
is juxtaposed, 'the cool appraising poise of the eulogy of Cromwell',
the 'disinterested concern with the object of contemplation', 'the
contemplating, relating and appraising mind' is what its 'strength
as feeling and attitude' depends on.[47]

By focusing on a few passages in these essays, where Leavis is
more explicit than usual about the critical concepts he employs, I
have tried to offer some leads about the way the concepts interpenetrate. I have tried to illustrate that what Leavis achieves by
employing his terms to some extent co-extensively is always to
imply that a poem is a totality when making particular emphases

about particular aspects or features of its working. The recession of the terms into one another helps to obviate the danger of tearing 'features' or 'effects' from the complex emotional-verbal-intellectual fabric of a poem.

(d) Enactment and realization: the signs of something grasped and held

Peter Barry has recently challenged Leavis' analysis of the passage from Keats' 'Ode to Autumn' in which he refers to the enactment of the balancing movement of the gleaner (see above, p. 51). Barry's paper is of particular interest since it seeks to question 'the doctrine of the organic fusion of form and content' which, according to Barry, made it 'obligatory to see formal details as intimately connected with content, since they had to enact meaning if they were not to be puritanically condemned as merely decorative'.[48]

Barry effectively demonstrates that many critics are guilty of over-eagerness and confusion in their hunt for enactment in poetry and his climactic example is Leavis' analysis of Keats' lines,

> And sometimes like a gleaner thou dost keep
> Steady thy laden head across a brook.

Leavis comments: 'In the step from the rime-word "keep" across (so to speak) the pause enforced by the line division, to "steady" the balancing movement of the gleaner is enacted.' Barry asks, 'how can a *pause* enact a movement? And is there really a pause at all in a line as vigorously run-on as this, except to the eye? Surely the words *describe* the act of balancing in spite of the assertion that Keats's verse transcends description, and the perceived enactment of balancing is quite subjective on Leavis's part.'[49] In the next chapter I will consider at some length the notions of subjectivity and objectivity in relation to critical argument. Barry's mode of reasoning is a good example of what I will refer to as dialectical or interpretative reasoning in criticism. The questions he asks invite assent but, of course, dissent is possible and, in this case, necessary. Leavis' point needs development, not rejection. The 'balancing movement' of the gleaner is *both* pause and movement. The bodily check to keep the 'laden head' steady is immediately followed by a pose of arrested motion as the balance is held. There *is* a tendency to 'vigorous run-on' in the lines at the same time as the eye attends to the oddity of dividing 'keep' from 'steady' by the line division. The lines thus enact the tension between movement and pause involved in the balancing.

Barry allows that, in general, Leavis' use of 'enactment' in his critical practice is subtle and cogent. In particular he finds Leavis' account of enactment in Donne's poetry to be convincing. (Leavis refers to 'the liveliness of enactment – something fairly to be called dramatic' in Donne's poetry, claiming that the poet achieves a fine 'mimetic flexibility', in which nuances of mood are 'echoed' by variations in pace and emphasis.) Barry concedes that Leavis does successfully demonstrate the interaction of form and content in the case of Donne's 'Satyre III' :

> Is not our Mistresse faire Religion,
> As worthy of all our soules devotion,
> As Vertue was to the first blinded age?
> Are not heavens joyes as valiant to asswage
> Lusts, as earth's honour was to them?

Leavis writes that if 'asswage' had not been a rhyme-word there would not have been quite that lagging deliberation of stress upon 'Lusts'; hence the rhyme is 'strictly used'. According to Barry, however, 'the only difficulty with this is the implicit criticism of all the other rhymes in the poem for not being quite so strictly used, since the implied ideal for rhyme is that it always be functional'.[50] Presumably Barry would make a similar claim about Leavis' example of enactment in Keats – that to point out the way the line division is 'strictly *used*' is an implicit criticism of all the other line divisions in the poem for not being so strictly used.

But pointing out one kind of strength does not imply that everything else is weakness. Barry mistakenly assumes that Leavis' conception of the 'functions' or 'uses' of line division, rhyme, imagery, movement, etc. in poetry is a narrow one, determined by rigidly held 'ideals' concerning the interaction of form and content. But, as I have pointed out in some detail, Leavis sees the 'functions' of these 'elements' to be extraordinarily various. Realization (and enactment) is 'one kind of thing in this poem and another in that, and within the poem, the relation of imagery [or movement or thought or feeling or rhythm or line division] to the whole involves complex possibilities of variety'.[51] Enactment of the kind that Leavis points to in Keats' poem is significantly different from the enactment he identifies in Donne. But in each case he is seeing the formal details as intimately connected with content and argues the superiority of poetry which does thus organically 'fuse' form and content over poetry which is merely decorative.

Leavis' recognition of the very wide range of ways and objects of realization in poetry makes it the most flexible term in his critical vocabulary. I noted earlier the 'sensuous realization' which Leavis holds to be characteristic of Keats' poetry – and of course the examples of enactment in Keats and Donne which I have been discussing are also forms of realization. I considered, as well, Leavis' account of Blake's realization, in a peculiarly visual way, of his inner vision. The major difficulty in generalizing about critical concepts as Leavis employs them – that they interpenetrate as do the aspects of a poem – is particularly acute with regard to 'realization'. For as Leavis employs the term it may apply to any of the myriad ways in which works of literature may be said to 'grasp' and 'hold' reality. Each of the examples he selects in the essays I examined (in section (c) above), from Blake, Keats, Tennyson, Lawrence and Marvell, reveal distinctive, often unexpected modes of realization in their verse. The critic has to be alert to the new demands which significant literary works may make on our conceptions of imagery, thought, feeling, movement, etc. and the ways in which these 'aspects' of a poem may be distinctively integrated or orchestrated to create the realization demanded, by Leavis, of the poet.

When Leavis defines 'realization', in *Education and the University*,[52] he insists that it is not a simple or an easily applied concept. The passage from *Macbeth* which he selects to exemplify 'realization' is that which I cited earlier, where the metaphor of a river is touched off by the words 'deep and broad'.[53] Leavis chooses this example in order to demonstrate that 'realization' can encompass almost the opposite of what it seems, superficially, to refer to. An apparent *failure* to make thoughts, feelings and images fully real is taken by Leavis as a notable example of realization. That which is 'realized, not merely verbal' is that which is felt and sensed as well as thought – 'whether we tell ourselves so or not, the presence of a river makes itself *felt* . . . giving a physical quality to "contend" '. Leavis' main point in his definition of 'realization' is that it cannot be used as a 'technical term' in the sense of being a 'simple or easily applied criterion'. 'It is in the incomplete realization of the metaphor that the realizing gift and the "realized" quality of the passage are manifested.' 'However we apply the term, what we have to consider is a whole of some complexity; what we have to look for are the signs of something grasped and held, and not merely thought of or gestured towards.'[54] Henry James observed that 'in proportion as [a literary work] lives will it be found that in each of the parts there is something of each of the other parts'. Leavis' criticism is designed to demonstrate that only when a work 'lives' in this way is 'realization' possible. Only when the 'parts' partake of one another and animate one another, when 'form' is thus inseparable from 'content', is anything 'made real' in literature – the alternative, as Leavis points out, is merely 'talking about'.

But of course the 'reality' that literature presents is not the reality of life, of full concrete actuality. Leavis suggests that poems come 'somewhere between full concrete actuality and merely "talking about" '. 'In reading a successful poem it is as if, with the kind of qualification intimated, one were living that particular action, situation or piece of life, the qualification representing the condition of the peculiar completeness and fineness of art.'[55] The 'reality' of literature is that of a constructed world in which we respond to representations or portrayals of characters, thoughts, events and so on. This world, because it is a created world, has a completeness and fineness which is absent from life in the real world, which is not ordered and shaped but is subject to chance and is full of loose ends. In the following chapters I will develop further this contrast between the perceptions and feelings which are occasioned by literature and the perceptions and feelings which are a consequence of our interaction with real people and real events. For unless the 'reality' of literature is clearly seen to be fundamentally distinct from the 'reality' of life it is impossible to avoid fundamental misconceptions about the objectives of literary education.

Although I have cited Leavis as having a clear view of this distinction it must be acknowledged that he sometimes loses sight of it in ways that could seriously mislead his readers. In chapter i I rejected the view which is sometimes to be found among English teachers that if children are to write 'sincere' poems and stories they should deal with their own personal experiences. Leavis some-times discusses major writers as if the realization of experience in their work depended upon the occurrence of actual experiences in their lives.

(e) Real experience and realization in literature

I want to refer again to T. S. Eliot's comments on the complex relations between literature and reality,[56] comments which point to the need for extreme caution in drawing a 'correspondence' between literature and anything outside itself, including the poet's experience. (The poet's experience 'may only exist . . . in the expression of it'.) Leavis sometimes commits himself to a position which is quite at odds with Eliot's point and with his own position as I have just outlined it. He sometimes maintains that whether or not a poet actually had real life experiences which give rise to his poems is an important source and test of their value. In 'Reality and sincerity', for example, he argues that Hardy was able to realize his experience in 'After a Journey' because he had really in life undergone experiences that the poem recounts.[57] Leavis simply takes the truth of this to be indubitable, but I can see no reason why, even if Hardy had undergone such actual experiences, we should assume that this is necessarily related to the superiority or inferiority of this or any poem in which there is no correspondence of the kind which Leavis asserts here between the 'reality' of the poem and the real life of the poet. Leavis leaves too little room, in this example and in others, for the possibility that the poet is entertaining imagined experience and that it is possible for the poet to 'make real' something that he never actually experienced.

Leavis' account of Tennyson's 'Tears, Idle Tears', in ' "Thought" and emotional quality', is in some respects inadequate because he is unwilling to allow that the speaker in the poem is not Tennyson inadequately realizing his own personal experience (or the lack of it). Cleanth Brooks maintains that 'the looseness and *apparent* confusion of unpremeditated speech' in the poem are 'very tightly organized'. 'It represents an organic structure and the intensity of the total effect is a reflection of the total structure.'[58]

If this poem were merely a gently melancholic reverie on the sweet sadness of the past, stanzas II and III would have no place in the poem. But the poem is no such reverie: the images from the past rise up with a strange clarity and sharpness which shock the speaker. Their sharpness and freshness account for the sudden fears and for the psychological problem with which the speaker wrestles in the poem. If the past would only remain melancholy but dimmed, sad but worn and familiar, we should have no problem and no poem. At least we should not have *this* poem; we should certainly not have the intensity of the last stanza.[59]

This account is completely at odds with Leavis' interpretation, and although I think that Brooks overstates his case (I don't, for example, find as much intensity in the poem as he does) there are certainly aspects of the poem to which Leavis does not attend and I think that this is at least partly because he does not allow for the possibility that Tennyson is not dramatizing his own personal experience. (Whether one judges the dramatization of the *speaker's* experience to be realized or not depends on how convincing one finds Brooks' interpretation.)

On the other hand there is, in apparent support of Leavis' approach to the poem, the fact that Tennyson said of it, 'The passion of the past, the abiding in the transient, was expressed in *Tears, Idle Tears*, which was written in the yellowing autumn-tide at Tintern Abbey, full for me of its bygone memories.'[60] Graham Hough comments that 'the memories could be historical ones, naturally called up by a monastic ruin; but in fact they seem to link the poem with "In Memoriam" 19, also said to have been written at Tintern Abbey . . . whose theme is Arthur Hallam's burial at Clevedon close by'.[61] However, Hough maintains that 'in the growth of this poem, the specific past has lost its private associations and the passion has ceased to be any private grief'.

Tennyson's note equates 'the passion of the past' with 'the abiding in the transient'. The transient is events, objects which were once present and are now past: the abiding is the essence of these events, presented to the mind as a passion, as a memory charged with emotion – but not reducible to longing, regret, sense of loss, or any specifiable emotion . . . The sense of dereliction . . . formed a tangled and aching knot somewhere deep in Tennyson's being, a small patch of death in the midst of his life . . . [Tennyson] sometimes . . . so orders [such] private and morbid emotions that they come to correspond with the general experience of the human species.[62]

I think that Hough overrates the extent to which 'Tears, Idle Tears' succeeds in realizing its emotions. I don't find the imagery to be 'poignant' and I find most peculiar Hough's comment that 'the pathos of autumn, of parting, of death, of hopeless love, all the things which make you want to cry' are 'all obvious and powerful sources of irremediable pain'. It is as if Hough *sees* that these are also obvious tear-jerkers, and it is because they come too close to being so in Tennyson's poem that I feel no impulse whatever to cry and do not find them 'powerful'.

Similarly, when Brooks claims that 'the images from the past rise up with a strange clarity and sharpness that shock the speaker', this seems to me to be so only in the sense that it points out the ostensible (not the realized) dramatic or psychological development of the poem – I don't think that the images *are* remarkable for either their freshness or their sharpness. And everything turns on this – the extent to which the poem *does* order private and morbid emotions so that they correspond with the general experience of the human species and the success of the dramatic or psychological development in the poem. If Leavis is right, and I think he is, that the images are only speciously particular and part of a current of vague emotion, then the poem ends up just being part of 'all the poetry about nostalgia and separation and about being dead when you don't want to be dead' as Hough so neatly (and inadvertently) puts it.

Nevertheless Brooks and Hough do see some possibilities in this poem that Leavis does not see, because Leavis sees the current of vague emotion as being *Tennyson's*. Whereas there is more evidence of 'thought' in the poem, particularly in its dramatic development, than Leavis allows. The poem does not *simply* 'offer emotion directly, emotion for its own sake'. There is an ordering of *some* complexity in the poem. The reader is not to be immersed 'wholly in and of the experience' as Leavis maintains, any more than Tennyson is 'wholly in or of it'. To recall Eliot's words again :

The poem's existence is somewhere between the writer and the reader; it has a reality which is not simply the reality of what the writer is trying to 'express' or of his experience in writing it or of the experience of the reader or of the writer as reader.

Leavis allows that for the *reader* of a successful poem it is '*as if* . . . one were living that particular action, situation or piece of life'. The qualification he inserts is an acknowledgement of the obvious distinction between 'image' and 'full concrete reality'. Poems come 'somewhere between full concrete actuality and merely "talking about" '.[63] But Leavis sometimes does not sufficiently allow that the writer may successfully offer imagined ('as if') experience that does not stem from his actual life. He does not sufficiently allow that 'the [writer's] experience may only exist in the expression of it'. It is this insufficiency which leads him to give unwarranted importance to his belief that Hardy was writing about his actual experience in 'After a Journey' and leads him to underestimate the dramatic subtlety of 'Tears, Idle Tears'.

The preceding discussions were primarily intended to bring out the immense variety and complexity of the relations between literary critical concepts. It would obviously be impossible, in the early stages of literary education, to expect students to develop a high degree of sensitivity towards the way in which, in successful literary works, 'what' is said is inseparable from 'the way it is said' and towards the ways in which 'aspects' such as imagery, plot, character, thought, feeling, rhythm, etc. are not traceable as a 'geography of items' but 'partake of one another' to form a whole. Nevertheless the temptation is strong, in the early stages, to provide clear definitions and cut-and-dried criteria, and this must inevitably lead to profound misconceptions of literary works, misconceptions which may be very difficult to dispel in later years. Unless the teacher is convinced that it is fatal to the development of a student's appreciation of literary works to trace a geography of items or to try to pull out the 'content' from the 'form' of a good poem or novel then what will occur will be thoroughly mis-educative. Students will be inclined to treat literary works as merely elaborate and complicated ways of dressing up ideas that could easily be expressed in other words.

Just how, with particular students, a teacher's handling of critical concepts might be informed by an awareness of the crucial interaction of form and content in literary works is obviously beyond my scope here. My aim has been simply to reinforce the teacher's belief that this is necessary if *any* discussion of literature occurs in the classroom or in tutorials. For any discussion may promote fundamental misconceptions of the distinctive 'voice' of literature in the 'conversation of mankind'.[64]

But, it may be objected, this is to assume far too much and to evade the most pressing problem. Who am I (who is Bradley, James, Eliot or Leavis) to declare that this is the way to approach the business of criticism or to declare that literary education should be informed by such an approach? Surely, it may be asserted, literary judgement is ultimately subjective. No one has the right to tell anyone else how they should go about reading books or how they should comment on them. On this account, literary evaluations are merely statements of personal preference. It is this challenge that I will try to meet in the next chapter.

3

Objectivity and subjectivity in literary education

It is the mark of an educated mind to expect that amount of exactness in each kind which the nature of the particular subject admits. It is equally unreasonable to accept merely probable conclusions from a mathematician and to demand strict demonstration from an orator.

(Aristotle)

It is not a simple matter to reply to the student who says, 'Look, I can see all your reasons for saying that Shakespeare is better than James Bond but I *like* reading James Bond more than Shakespeare.' The student may defend his preference by saying that James Bond is easier to read, identification with the hero is much simpler, it's more exciting, and so on. Many teachers find themselves in the rather embarrassing position of secretly sharing the student's preference for 'a good read' but feel obliged to press a case for Shakespeare which they may not strongly feel at all. This often produces in literature teachers a kind of guilt or a feeling of hypocrisy. After a hard day at school the teacher may well be disinclined to read Shakespeare – all he may want to do is 'escape' into James Bond or television.

There is, of course, nothing hypocritical about this. When we want to relax, or 'turn off', our most easily satisfied tastes and preferences are often quite naturally the dominant ones : the danger remains, however, that the teacher may develop a kind of cynicism about introducing students to great literature when he feels that much of the time he himself *prefers* the second- or third-rate. This is particularly likely to be a problem if it is associated with the belief that while other teachers (of science, history or mathematics for example) have objective procedures and standards which enable them to assess or examine their students' work, arguments about literary matters are merely rationalizations for personal preferences rather than reasons that establish objective conclusions.

Some distinguished philosophers lend support to the teacher's doubts about the objectivity of critical judgements and procedures. Since I take it that one of the distinguishing features of an educative activity (as distinct from indoctrination on the one hand and idle chat on the other) is a concern for objectivity of judgement, it is important that these doubts be examined.

Margaret Macdonald[1] has argued that all that can be hoped for in criticism are 'better' or 'worse' judgements. 'No critic, even the best, is infallible. . .' However, I think we can safely assume that objectivity does not imply infallibility and that an objective judgement need not be beyond the *possibility* of error. If no one (on earth !) is infallible, objectivity in Macdonald's account would be impossible. If objectivity is impossible it seems absurd to isolate literary criticism for special attention.

It is widely believed, nevertheless, that in some respects mathematics and science are unchallengeable or beyond the possibility of doubt in ways that criticism never could be :

> criticism does not, and cannot, have the impersonal character and strict rules applicable independently of time and place, appropriate to science and mathematics. A mathematician who claimed to have squared the circle, a scientist who announced a law for which he could give no empirical evidence, would be justly ridiculed. But to attempt to legislate for the arts is to invite the infringement of any law.[2]

Neither of Macdonald's examples establishes a contrast with criticism which demonstrates its lack of objectivity. The mathematical claim is a logical impossibility. No amount of testing could persuade us of the possibility of squaring the circle. This is inconceivable and unintelligible. To say that a judgement is not objective because it is unintelligible is most misleading. References to square circles do not lack objectivity, they lack intelligibility. Intelligibility is a precondition of objectivity. Certainly it is true that an unintelligible utterance cannot be an objective judgement. But this is because its lack of intelligibility means that it is not even decipherable as a *judgement*. Needless to say, literary critical utterances which are unintelligible or self-contradictory would also be 'justly ridiculed'.

  If the scientist's claim is that the principle for establishing a law in science is that he announces it, this is no less irrational than a literary critic's claim that the principle for establishing a literary

judgement is that he announces it. It is no more, and no less, irrational to make claims to knowledge in science without evidence
than it is in any other form of discourse.

It is significant that Macdonald does not offer an example of a
scientific judgement which could be said to be beyond doubt/
certain/infallible and thus 'objective'. As John Casey points out,
'If a man insists on describing something as being like *this*, despite
all the evidence we bring that it is like *that*, there may be little we
can do – but this would be the position in science as well as in
aesthetics.'[3] Observers of the sun at Fatima were undisturbed by
the scientific evidence to the effect that the sun cannot dip down
to the horizon and back again in a few minutes. Members of the
Flat Earth Society are undisturbed by scientific evidence of the
shape of the earth (though there was a falling off of membership
when the first satellite pictures were transmitted to earth. But it
was not long before the exponent of the flat earth theory outside
the Melbourne Public Library was back with detailed explanations
of how this 'illusion' was produced).

Toulmin points out that the more strictly 'theoretical' is a term
in science, 'the more conditional, hypothetical and indirect is its
application to individual objects identified here and now'. The
more theoretical is a statement in science, the more its empirical
relevance is a matter of 'applicability' rather than of 'truth'.

In the course of establishing the conditions on which any explanatory
technique can be successfully applied, a scientist determines (i) in what
empirical situations the propositions of the corresponding theory hold
good – not whether they are 'true' – and (ii) what empirical objects or
systems count as – rather than 'are' – instances of the corresponding
theoretical entities.[4]

According to Toulmin it is 'explanatory power' rather than direct
'empirical truth' which constitutes the 'intellectual substance' of a
natural science.

When the empiricist's back is to the wall he will usually start
talking about the furniture : 'My seeing a table, you seeing a table,
etc., does enable us to say that a table is there.'[5] Such propositions
seem to be paradigms of 'objectivity' and are fundamental to our
belief that there is a world of material objects outside ourselves to
which empirical assertions refer and by reference to which they
may be 'objectively' settled. No critical judgement has the direct

relationship to what is observed that characterizes 'this is a chair', 'this is my hand'. I want to make two points about this.

1. Wittgenstein asks if the certainty we attach to such propositions is an empirical certainty.

306. 'I don't know if this is a hand'. But do you know what the word hand means? And don't say 'I know what it means now for me'. And isn't it an empirical fact – that this word is used like *that*?

307. And here the strange thing is that when I am quite certain of how the words are used, have no doubt about it, I can still give no *grounds* for my way of going on. If I tried I could give a thousand but none as certain as the very thing they were supposed to be grounds for.

308. . . . about certain empirical propositions no doubt can exist if making judgements is to be possible at all. Or again, I am inclined to believe that not everything that has the form of an empirical proposition *is* one.[6]

We may not know what a chair or a hand is (if we are a very small child, for example) but when we do know what is meant it is absurd to ask for *evidence* for 'this is a hand' or 'this is a chair'. Claiming empirical knowledge *presupposes* that we can refer to direct observation statements as grounds. Such propositions are not themselves empirically or scientifically verifiable – they have a certainty which indicates their logical necessity as presuppositions of discourse. If someone were to say, 'I do not know if this is a hand before me' or 'I do not know if this is a chair which you are seeing and I am seeing' we would not take him to mean that he was doubting its existence, unless there were special circumstances such as an L.S.D. party or a mirror maze. We would have to assume that he lacked an understanding of what 'chair' or 'hand' means, as in the case of someone just learning the language. In this respect, since it seems absurd to speak of *proving* such propositions as 'this is my hand', direct observation statements are more closely related to logically necessary propositions such as 'the angles of a triangle add up to $180°$'. Someone who was unable to see this might believe himself to be doubting an empirical proposition – he may have measured lots of triangles and found that their angles added up to $179°$. But no amount of measuring could cast doubt on the proposition that the sum of the angles of a triangle is $180°$, for that is part of what is meant by 'triangle'.

Critical judgements could not be certain in the way that such propositions about triangles are, nor in the way that statements of direct observation may be. But in so far as such propositions could not be doubted it would seem that they are preconditions of objective judgements rather than being themselves objective judgements. To doubt them is to misunderstand them, not to challenge the judgement. There is a kind of unintelligibility about 'This triangle adds up to 179°' as there may also be about 'this is not my hand'. And it is misleading to maintain that the presence of intelligibility ('This triangle adds up to 180°'; 'This is my hand') is what is meant by objectivity.

2. Even if I managed to persuade the empiricist of this, he might still say that even if statements of direct observation could not themselves be said to be objective judgements, I have acknowledged that they may be said to be indubitable. Judgements in science which rest on these may be said to be objective in a way that literary critical judgements could never be, since what is often contentious is just what characteristics are actually possessed, as a matter of observation, by a work of literature. Even when agreement is reached it is merely agreement – it never depends on reference back to what is indubitable.

However, I think that objectivity need not involve objects, even in empirical matters. Professor Sibley has pointed out that in the case of colour judgements, 'there is only direct appeal to agreement'.[7] Of course, not just any agreement will do. When people say that the only ultimate way to find out the colour of something is to 'look and see', they mean 'under the right conditions' (good light, etc.) and with the right kind of viewer (not one who is colour blind, dazzled, etc.). Similarly, when we say of aesthetic features, 'either one just sees or one doesn't', we may assume certain conditions obtain, for example that the reader or the viewer does not lack the relevant experience, knowledge, linguistic skills, etc. For without these it may be the case that one just cannot 'see'. It would be inappropriate to say of a child who has read *Antony and Cleopatra*, and who fails to see the way Antony and Cleopatra feed on one another and sap each other's wills (and the way the 'appetite' imagery in the play realizes this) that either one just sees or one doesn't. For there are good reasons to think that a young child just could not see these features of the play.

Although there may be less widespread agreement about aesthetic features than there is about colours this could be attributed to the immensely more complex demands which poems and paintings make on the reader or viewer. As a consequence of these demands there may be a much smaller group (a 'nucleus' or an 'elite' as Sibley calls them) whose perception of aesthetic features is 'reliable' (in the sense that they tend to agree on many more detailed discriminations, similarities, differences, etc. than others ever do). Sibley points out that if there were, in fact, a much smaller group of 'reliable' colour discriminators this need not seriously threaten the objectivity of colours.[8]

I do not want to deny a fundamental difference between chairs and galaxies, on the one hand, and works of literature, on the other. Chairs and galaxies have an objective existence (exist as objects) independent of our interpretation or understanding of them, whereas works of literature exist 'somewhere between the reader and the writer'. Unlike chairs and galaxies, which simply *are*, works of literature *mean*. The only respect in which a poem has an objective existence like that of chairs and galaxies is as black marks on white paper.

This difference does not lead, however, to a distinction between the objectivity of our *knowledge* of the nature of chairs and galaxies and of our knowledge of the nature of works of literature. None of our knowledge of the nature of chairs and galaxies could, logically, be independent of the interpretative conceptual apparatus we bring to bear in making judgements about chairs and galaxies. What they *are* like, independent of such an interpretative framework, is obviously unknowable (though we do not doubt that they do *have* such an independent existence).

I think that this is an important point so I will run the risk of labouring it and put it slightly differently. Since poems are structures of *meaning* it makes no sense to consider their existence independently of our interpretation of them (except as black marks on white paper). But it does not follow from this that our knowledge of the nature of a poem need be less objective than our knowledge of the nature of a chair or of a galaxy. No direct knowledge of the nature of anything is possible since all observations and judgements are possible only within an interpretative framework. The nature of chairs and galaxies, no less than of works of literature, is a matter of interpretation and there is no a priori reason why the means of determining the nature of one need be more or less subjective or objective than the means of determining the nature of the other.

In short, our conviction that chairs and galaxies have an objective *existence* in a way that poems do not offers no support for the view that *judgements* about the former are more objective than judgements about the latter.

I will conclude this examination of a variety of arguments which have been advanced by philosophers to support the view that judgements and procedures in fields such as science and mathematics are objective (and thus to be contrasted with the subjectivity of critical procedures and judgements) by referring to Michael Scriven's conclusions in his paper, 'The objectivity of aesthetic evaluation' : 'In short, the "scientific model" of justification cannot be applied to aesthetic evaluation – and it appears to be the only one which can give any objective foundation for that activity.'[9] Scriven's conclusion is puzzling since he rejects the view that it is necessary for the critic to argue in the way (on one model of scientific justification) scientists argue :

> The idea that logic requires us to derive our reasons from precise generalizations is especially misleading in art where precise generalizations are very hard to find and even harder to pin down to a particular case. It is often true that we feel more confident of the merit-rating of a particular work of art than of any precise generalization.[10]

However, the 'scientific model' Scriven has in mind is that of the applied sciences : 'in the applied sciences there is little dispute about the identification of the advantageous qualities (strength of structural material, durability of finishes, economy etc.)'.[11] Scriven maintains that it is easy to prove that these qualities just *are* advantageous in a way that is not possible in discussions of the qualities of works of art.

I think that an answer to Scriven is implied in an article by John Wilson when he discusses what makes a move in chess elegant. 'The "appreciation" of the "reasons" comes purely from criteria within the game; rather like "elegant" solutions by architects to problems posed by stresses and strains, the materials they have available and so on, such as the flying buttress.'[12] The architect draws on his knowledge of the applied sciences, e.g. concerning strength of structural material, durability, economy, etc. and relates it to the knowledge that the flying buttress will create a soaring effect on the outside of a cathedral and permit the height of the nave to be dramatically increased so that a sense of awe and mystery will pervade the building.

But is the 'knowledge' of these religious/aesthetic effects

objective, Scriven might well ask. Well, there is no doubt that the cathedral architects thought so – they were prepared to sacrifice economy, for example, on a grand scale in order to achieve the religious/aesthetic effects. They were even prepared to take enormous risks with strength of structural material in order to achieve such effects. (The roof of the nave of Beauvais cathedral is awesome – the highest in Europe – and it collapsed on an Easter day last century.)

Scriven might return that at least the objective *test* of durability is available – the roof either falls in or it doesn't, whereas whether or not a flying buttress is 'soaringly beautiful' or a nave awesome and mysterious is not similarly testable.

It is true that the tests for the latter are not of the same *kind*, but this is not to say that they are not objective. Let me return to Wilson's comments on what makes a move in chess elegant. The 'appreciation' of the 'reasons', says Wilson, comes purely from criteria within the game. So that,

> Anyone who had a deep understanding of chess (1) could hardly help 'appreciating' the merits of the move,[13] and (2) would express this *just by* pointing out (if asked) why it was so good. ('Don't you see, it gets his king out of trouble while simultaneously threatening mate in three ways and forking the queen. . .' and so on). What else could we want from him?[14]

Of course works of literature are very different from games of chess, but the mode of reasoning Wilson employs in order to argue that a move in chess is elegant, and which a number of philosophers have referred to as 'dialectical' or 'interpretative' reasoning, is characteristic of critical argument.[15] There is an implicit question–answer form to Wilson's argument – 'Don't you see?' : 'What else could you want?' – which does not rely on *general* norms or standards of elegance of which this particular move is an instance but, instead, asks of a particular move, 'If *this* is not elegant, what on earth could be meant by an elegant move in chess?' It is *conceivable* that we might reply with a counter-instance described in such a way that weaknesses in Wilson's account might become apparent, though what this might be is not easy to see.

This mode of reasoning bears a close resemblance to a great deal of literary critical argument, most explicitly in the case of F. R. Leavis. When he offers an account of what, in a particular work of literature, makes it 'realized' or how, in another work, the 'parts' interpenetrate to form a 'whole', he typically uses a questioning, comparative technique – 'This is how "imagery" relates to "thought" in this work, isn't it?' 'Compare it with this work, where imagery and thought fail to partake of one another, to the detriment of the work, wouldn't you agree?' Leavis, we saw, does not invite (in fact goes out of his way to avoid) argument on a *general* level about what is imagery, thought, movement, feeling, etc. in literature and how these aspects interrelate in good literature, just as he refuses to offer general definitions of key terms of evaluation such as 'realization'.

Peter Byrne has recently pointed out that to be able to *apply* any general definition of such terms

would involve just that ability to handle and discriminate among particular cases, just that refinement and delicacy in perception, which was needed to apply the term defined. We should still be left with judgement which went beyond the reports of simple observation but which nevertheless could not be justified by appeal to general principles.[16]

The critic displays the meaning of his terms by showing how they discriminate among particular cases.[17]

No body of general critical principles could be clearly understood 'unless one had a prior grasp of the concrete judgements they were supposed to justify'. Thus, the general principle which we have observed to be operative in the work of the diverse group of critics to which we have referred in chapter 2, concerning the relationship between 'form' and 'content' in literature, is not used to *justify* particular judgements about literary works – it requires critical judgement to be applied and interpreted. As R. Peacock points out, aesthetic principles are generalizations based on judgements *already made* about the selected examples taken to be art.[18]

A number of writers have pointed out the resemblance between Leavis' mode of reasoning and that of philosophers such as Socrates, Wisdom and Wittgenstein. John Casey, whose work is profoundly influenced by both Leavis and Wittgenstein, exhibits the approach in the following passage:

Someone may accept the analysis of a poem as, say, weak in realization, and by the same token sentimental, and by the same token unintelligent, but still refuse to accept that it is bad. If he goes through this process of evaluation with us, and yet refuses to admit that what he has agreed to adds up to saying that the poem is a bad one, he is still not contradicting himself. We might, however, wonder what he is saying; we might wonder if he has the concept of evaluation. Similarly he might refuse any one of the steps in the evaluative process. . . If, however many sentimental-making features we pointed out, he persists in his denial (without giving cogent reasons) we cannot convict him of contradiction, although we may be permitted to wonder what, if anything, he *is* saying, and whether he *has* the concept of sentimentality.[19]

In his discussion of Leavis' criticism Casey emphasizes the way in which Leavis' mode of critical argument establishes links between description and evaluation. The dichotomy between facts and values is often the bedrock of the dichotomy between those areas of discourse which are alleged to be objective (concerned with facts) and those which are alleged to be subjective (concerned with values). It is quite usual for English teachers to refer to literary judgements (and moral judgements) as 'just' or 'merely' value judgements. It is common in my experience of student teachers to hear a good critical account of a poem or novel followed up with the disclaimer, 'Of course, it's only my (personal) value-judge-ment.' One unfortunate consequence of this is that teachers often spend much of their time dealing with 'factual' matters in litera-ture. 'Comprehension exercises' invite students to recall plot out-lines, character descriptions and so on, and the historical and biographical background to literary works is emphasized because at least knowledge (or recall) of this sort of material is 'objectively' assessable.

The history of the disjunction between (objective) matters of fact and (subjective) value judgements is a long one, but it has been most succinctly and influentially expressed by David Hume :

Morality consists . . . not in any *matter of fact* . . . morality is not an object of reason. Take any action allowed to be vicious : Wilful murder, for instance. Examine it in all lights and see if you can find that matter of fact, or real existence which you call *vice*. In whichever way you take it you find only certain passions, motives, volitions, and thoughts. There is no other matter of fact in the case. The vice entirely escapes you, as long as you consider the object. You never can find it, till you turn your reflection into your own breast, and find a sentiment of disapprobation, which arises in you towards this action. Here is a matter of fact; but 'tis the object of feeling, not of reason. It lies in yourself, not in the object. So that when you pronounce any action or character to be vicious, you mean nothing, but that from the constitution of your nature you have a feeling or sentiment of blame from the contemplation of it. . .

Where a passion is neither founded on false suppositions nor chuses means insufficient for the end, the understanding can neither justify nor condemn it. 'Tis not contrary to reason to prefer the destruction of the whole world to the scratching of my finger.[20]

Those who have followed Hume have regarded value judgements as matters of attitude, or taste, or emotional predilection, which may be psychologically explained but which are incapable of rational justification. Hume's point is that there can be no formal logical contradiction between the description of a fact and value judgements such as, 'You ought not to do *x, y* or *z*', 'It is bad to do *x, y* or *z*.'

In the passage we cited from John Casey a moment ago, Hume's point is acknowledged – even though what is being said sounds absurd or unintelligible it still falls short of self-contradiction. We could also expect Hugo Meynell, in the following passage, to concede that no formal contradiction occurs in any of the cases he cites:

If I say that a kind of chocolate is good, and that everyone who eats it is nauseated; if I say that a medicine is good, and it turns out to hasten death in all who use it; if I say that a man is good, when he deliberately causes as much misery as he can to all those who have anything to do with him; I am shown by the circumstances to be *objectively wrong* in my statements just as much as if I have described something as red all over which later observation has determined to be blue all over.[21]

Meynell is clearly allowing that no formal contradiction is involved in any of these cases (as there would be if I described something as red and blue all over at the same time). His point is that there may be conceptual connections between facts and values which, if ignored, lead to absurdity and unintelligibility. It is 'contrary to reason' to maintain that only self-contradiction is unreasonable. John Casey's argument makes the analogous point in the context of literary criticism.

But it is still possible, in the literary example, to say that one *likes* the poem (despite its being sentimental, unintelligent, etc.). Perhaps it reminds one of one's mother, maybe certain rhythms stir one's emotions, even though one knows that these are irrelevant in the context of the poem; everyone has tastes and preferences which *are* personal, idiosyncratic and subjective. Even among literary works which we have no doubt are major works there are wide discrepancies between what people like or prefer to read. As Peacock maintains,

Everything concerning subject, materials and ideas in a work includes interests and values that stretch from the simpler levels of sensuous reaction to the complicated ones of intellectual, emotional and moral character and all these vary from individual to individual in patterns of great complexity, making taste partly subjective and variable, and in consequence giving the basis for the relativist position in criticism.[22]

For it is what you are full of, what haunts you, what pushes your thoughts and feelings in certain directions and won't let go, that determines what you write; and also determines what readers read with greater or lesser interest.[23]

Similarly, people vary immensely in their personal predilections for poetry or the novel, for literature which explores religion or personal relations or social affairs. Peacock argues that

To a reader in sympathy with an author's belief or subject, his poem or work means more; not as bare belief but as poem including the belief . . . if some factors in a work run counter to a person's tastes or interests, that work ceases, to that extent, to *function*, as an art work, for that person. Its impact, effect, influence are reduced; it does less for one. What is involved here is taste and value response, not a logic of critical criteria or standards.[24]

The pedagogical implications of this are obvious. Just *what* literature one teaches to whom will depend partly on eliciting the tastes and preferences of the students. (Though of course one need not merely *cater* to the taste of one's students – teachers are characteristically trying to develop new interests and preferences. Still, it is important that the teacher finds out what the existing tastes and preferences are, so that he can make an *informed* decision about whether or not to challenge the students with something different, or to work with literature which closely relates to their interests and preferences.)

There are methodological issues of such particularity here that they cannot be developed within the scope of this book. I have been concerned, however, with a 'logic of critical criteria or standards', though what I have offered is certainly not as cut and dried as Peacock's phrase suggests. This attempt has been made partly in response to what Peacock says is

almost a conspiracy to leave the problem of objective values and criteria severely alone. . . . The predominant practical attitude is permissive, if one may borrow an ethical analogy from other spheres of present day life. People are generously allowed their 'opinion', and above all their 'right' to have personal opinions. And one reserves the right to have one's own principles, without foisting them on to others, and also without being in any hurry to define or declare them.[25]

The climate of opinion to which Peacock refers is an influential one among those concerned with teaching literature. Part of the reason why no one is in any hurry to confront the problem of objective procedures and values in literary discussion is that they are extremely elusive and, for reasons I have tried to elucidate, highly unsusceptible to definition. In fact, I have argued, the principles are dependent for their meaning on discussions of particular works of literature.

To some this may seem so unlike objective procedures in other fields that it may confirm all their worst suspicions about the claims of literary criticism to be much more than chatting about books. Let me conclude, then, with a passage from Peter Byrne's stimulating paper when he combats the sceptical doubts raised by the fact that 'in criticism, firstly, disputes cannot be settled by further observations; and secondly . . . there is no body of general principles by means of which the answer may be deduced from the observations'. Byrne refers to the work of John Wisdom, who provides a philosophical defence of the idea that reasoning by means of the direct discussion of concrete examples may be a 'cogent alternative to reasoning in terms of general principles'.

Wisdom finds such cases in many fields: e.g. in the law, in theology, in philosophy. Thus to take a legal example: counsel may disagree whether the action of a defendant constituted negligence. This may be so even though they accept the evidence concerning the defendant's actions. They may still argue whether these actions constitute negligence despite the fact that there may be no general principles which lay down when a course of action amounts or does not amount to negligence. In the absence of agreed principles we can imagine argument proceeding by reference to parallel cases. By way of settling the question we can imagine the parties lighting upon an admitted case of negligence and considering how like in the relevant respects this case is. This can proceed by exhibiting or contrasting parallel or intermediate cases which are admitted not to be cases of negligence. To see the course of action as a case of negligence is to see it as being one with certain others, as being along a line with them, but as contrasting with yet further cases. As Leavis says, one enforces judgement by locating the case in question in a map or chart of other relevant cases and one invites comment on the pattern one has thus committed oneself to.[26]

Byrne concludes that reasoning in terms of parallel cases is not to be seen as necessarily inferior to reasoning in terms of general principles and that consequently literary criticism need not suffer on this count by comparison with other humane disciplines.

4

The subordination of criticism to theory: structuralism and deconstructionism

I have attempted to characterize some of the distinctive concepts and procedures of literary criticism and to defend the activity against a variety of misconceptions. I have suggested that some of these misconceptions are a result of the reluctance of literary critics to be articulate about the nature of their pursuit. Uncertainty about the justification for criticism has helped to enable the widespread circulation of structuralist and post-structuralist approaches to literature.

Jonathan Culler, in *Structuralist Poetics*, observes that 'few of the many who write about literature have the desire or arguments to defend their activity. . . If the role criticism has been called upon to play in the educational system serves to explain the quantity of critical writings it does little to justify the activity itself.'[1] Culler aims to make out a case for criticism as 'an independent mode of knowledge', 'a coherent discipline' and to do so he turns to the model of linguistics.

The linguistic model . . . helped [French critics] to justify the desire to abandon literary history and biographical criticism . . . the conclusion that literature could be studied as 'a system with its own order' has been enormously salutary, securing for the French some of the benefits of Anglo-American 'New Criticism' without leading to the error of making the individual text an autonomous object that should be approached with a tabula rasa.[2]

According to Culler, criticism which focuses 'on the text itself', which 'prizes this encounter and the resulting interpretations' is 'more difficult to defend' than historical scholarship which was 'once the dominant mode of criticism'. Such scholarship could at least be defended as 'an attempt to bring supplementary and inaccessible information to bear on the text and thus to assist understanding'. Whereas 'interpretative criticism' cites 'no special knowledge which it deems to be crucial and from which it might derive its authority'.[3] It offers 'but a more thorough and perceptive version of what every reader does for himself'.[4] For literary study to be a discipline it requires, for Culler, the authority conferred by 'special knowledge' and this is not to be found in the perusal and discussion of individual works. 'The study of literature, as opposed to the perusal and discussion of individual works would become an attempt to understand the conventions which make literature possible.'[5] The study of such conventions provides the 'special knowledge' and 'supplementary and [otherwise] inaccessible information' which are essential for a 'discipline'.

Revealingly, Culler thinks that 'interpretative' critics secretly aspire to this kind of 'objectivity'. 'What critic does not in his moments [*sic*] dream of a scientifically rigorous way of characterizing the meaning of a text, of demonstrating with tools of proven appropriateness that certain meanings are possible and others impossible.'[6] This dream is unattainable, however, since critical interpretations are relative, according to Culler, to 'the conventions of reading poetry'.

Such conventions are the constituents of the institution of literature, and in this perspective one can see that it may well be misleading to speak of poems as harmonious totalities, autonomous natural organisms, complete in themselves and bearing a rich immanent meaning. The semiological approach suggests, rather, that the poem be thought of as an utterance that has meaning only with respect to a system of conventions which the reader has assimilated. If other conventions were operative its range of potential meanings would be different.[7]

The basic task for literary study is to construct a 'comprehensive theory of literary discourse'. In order to understand how literature works the literature student must set about 'formulating the broad laws of literary experience, and in short, writing as though he believed that there is a totally intelligible structure of knowledge attainable about poetry, which is not poetry itself, or the experience of it, but poetics'.[8] This quotation from Northrop Frye's *Anatomy of Criticism* is followed by another in which the model of science as the paradigm of a 'discipline' is even more explicit. According to Culler, 'if we are to make any sense at all of the process of literary education and of criticism itself, we must, as Frye argues, assume the possibilitiy of "a coherent and comprehensive theory of literature, logically and scientifically organized" '.[9]

In the preceding chapters I have argued that, on the contrary, sense can be made of literary education and criticism without assuming any such possibility. While Culler is right to point out that criticism has not been adequately defended as a discipline or as an educational activity, there were defences available when *Structuralist Poetics* was published, in particular those of F. R. Leavis and John Casey, to which I have referred. Criticism as they understand it is labelled 'traditionalist' and dismissed by caricature (e.g. it makes 'the individual text an autonomous object that should be approached with a tabula rasa'). Culler refers to the 'naive traditionalist critique' of structuralist poetics which 'asserts the uniqueness of the work of art and the inadmissibility of general theories' and which implies that 'the process of interpretation is random and haphazard'.

There is, of course, no reason to believe that the process of interpretation need be random and haphazard in the absence of general theories. On the contrary, criticism of the kind that I described earlier, which attempts to do justice to the complex interaction of form and content in literary works, necessitates a high degree of precision if this purpose is to be achieved.

However, it is not from 'traditionalist' critics that Culler sees any serious threat to his programme for structuralist poetics – they receive only a few dismissive comments of the kind I have cited. Culler is much more concerned to deal with the objections of those post-structuralist critics and theorists who, he anticipates, would condemn his semiological approach because he 'reifies' it as a 'science' and would accuse it of being 'ideological'. He refers to Julia Kristeva's views :

Semiotics cannot develop except as a critique of semiotics. . . Research in semiotics remains an investigation which discovers nothing at the end of its quest but its own ideological moves, so as to take cognizance of them, to deny them, and to start out anew.[10]

As Culler points out, a consequence of this argument is that there is no standpoint from which any proposal about the verbal structure of a text could be reached. 'In the absence of any primitive notion of the meanings or effects of a text . . . there is nothing to limit the play of meaning.'[11]

I will return in a moment to Culler's reference to a 'primitive' notion of the meanings or effects of a text since I think that his need to insist on this notion to protect himself from the absurdities of the 'radical' position undermines his attempt to make criticism merely 'ancillary' to poetics. Before I argue this, however, Culler's exposure of these absurdities is worth noting.

Anything can be related to anything else, certainly: a cow is like the third law of thermodynamics in that neither is a wastepaper basket, but little can be done with that fact. Other relations, however, do have thematic potential, and the crucial question is, what governs their selection and development. Even if 'emptied' by a radical theory the centre will inevitably fill itself in as the analyst makes choices and offers conclusions. There will always be some kind of semiotic or literary competence at work and the need for it will be greater if the range of relations with which it must deal is enlarged.[12]

Culler acknowledges that his opponents might accept this but say that the centre is never fixed but always constructed and deconstructed with a freedom which the 'radical' theorists seek as an end in itself. He rehearses his opponents' reply as follows:

If as Barthes and Foucault have shown, the argument might run, our social and cultural world is the product of various symbolic systems, should we not refuse any privileged status to the conventions erected by the oppressive institutions of the moment and joyfully claim for ourselves the right to produce meaning *ad libitum,* thus securing by the process of perpetual self-transcendence invulnerability to any criticism based on positivistic criteria and levelled at us from outside?[13]

Culler correctly points out that even if semiology refuses to 'reify' itself as a science it does not, for that, escape criticism : 'Whatever the past and future of the discipline, any particular analysis takes place at a particular stage, is an object with premises and results; and the possibility of denying these premises at the next moment does not make evaluation impossible or inappropriate.'[14] The range of meanings which a line of verse can bear depends on the fact that other meanings are manifestly impossible. Culler cites Barthes in his support : 'one can't make sense in any way whatsoever (if you don't believe me, try it)'.[15]

This point returns us to Culler's 'primitive notion of the meanings or effects of a text' which operates, for Culler, as 'a standpoint to limit the play of meaning'. This standpoint is crucial for Culler's rejection of 'radical' theories and also as the foundation of his structuralist poetics.

One starts with notions of the meaning or effects of a poem and tries to identify the structures responsible for those effects. Possible configurations or patterns which make no contribution are rejected as irrelevant.

That is to say, our intuitive understanding of the poem functions as the 'centre' governing the play of forms: it is both a starting point – what enables one to identify structures – and a limiting principle.[16]

At a number of earlier points in his book Culler has emphasized that structuralism enables an 'important reversal of perspective, granting precedence to the task of formulating a comprehensive theory of literary discourse and assigning a secondary place to the interpretation of individual texts'.[17] But when Culler is confronted with the challenge of the 'radicals' it is 'one's notions of the meanings and effects of a poem' with which one starts and it is this understanding which enables us to identify structures. Culler tries to reduce the significance of this admission by referring to this understanding as 'primitive' and 'intuitive'. But it is surely ill-advised to leave the starting point, centre, and limiting principle of one's structuralist analysis in a primitive or intuitive state. Why not refine it, develop it, check our understanding with that of other readers? Culler clearly does not want to do so because this is obviously to engage in 'interpretative criticism' in a way that makes it not merely 'ancillary' or 'secondary' to the task of 'formulating a comprehensive theory of literary discourse' but, instead, a determinant of the adequacy of the theory. If the understanding of a poem, which is the basis for the analysis of structures, is inadequate then the analysis becomes misguided.

Consider, for example, Culler's treatment of the final stanza of Shelley's 'The Cloud'.

> I am the daughter of Earth and Water,
>   And the nursling of the Sky;
> I pass through the pores of the ocean and shores;
>   I change, but I cannot die.
> For after the rain when with never a stain
>   The pavilion of Heaven is bare,
> And the winds and sunbeams with their convex gleams
>   Build up the blue dome of air
> I silently laugh at my own cenotaph,
>   And out of the caverns of rain
> Like a child from the womb, like a ghost from the tomb,
>   I arise and unbuild it again.

Donald Davie speaks of this as a poem 'ruined by licentious phrasing', by which he means a lack of semantic coherence: 'ocean and shores', for example, is, he claims, 'unthinkable in speech or prose'. We might go some way towards defending Shelley but we should, I think, be obliged to concede defeat in the end, for it is obvious that 'shores' is determined by the rhyme with 'pores', 'cenotaph' by the rhyme with 'laugh' and that there is no coherent cosmology at work here. 'Shelley pitches his poem in a high key, to advise us not to expect nicety of discrimination and prosaic sense', says Davie, and in those expectations we can see one convention of the lyric at work: the use of a prosodic and phonetic order to lift us away from empirical contexts and to impose another order which we can call, precisely, the sublime.

We naturalize such poems in a very formal and abstract way by showing how various features contribute to patterns which help to assert the monumentality and impersonality of poetry, but we can also provide a general context in which they become meaningful by saying that their job is to break out of the 'middle distance' of realism and to assert, as Wallace Stevens says, that 'gaiety of language is our seigneur' and that the making of fictions is a worthy activity.[18]

It is not easy to separate Culler's understanding of this verse from the (structuralist?) analysis he provides. The lead which Davie offers him, that the poem is 'ruined by licentious phrasing', is to a large extent lost when this becomes, blandly, 'a lack of semantic coherence'. But the 'concession of defeat' seems to indicate that Culler might recognize that the licentious phrasing is one aspect of a quality which pervades the verse, the perception of which is necessary to any adequate understanding of it and upon which the value of any 'structuralist' extrapolations depends. I refer, of course, to the puerility of the verse. Its rhythms and rhymes belong to the nursery. In fact the inclusion of verse such as this in anthologies for children is the sort of thing that turns children off poetry. It encourages them to think that poetry is trivial and silly, that poets don't worry too much about sense so long as they can get a rollicking rhythm and 'good' rhymes. They want to know why something unthinkable in speech or prose is acceptable in verse, they want to know why the cloud silently laughs at its own cenotaph, and they are not likely to be impressed by being told that expectations of nicety of discrimination and merely prosaic sense 'exhibit one convention of the lyric at work'. The prosodic and phonetic order of this verse does not 'lift us away' from empirical contexts, it simply blurs the failure of the language to grasp anything. I am not denying that in some manual of stylistic classification this verse might be called 'precisely, the sublime'. I am certainly denying that the verse breaks out of the 'middle distance' of realism to assert that 'gaiety of language is our seigneur' and that the making of fictions is a worthy activity.

Culler elsewhere shows an awareness of the dangers of overinflated structuralist readings which, seeking support for a 'theory' of literature, make gross errors of judgement.

If a poem seems utterly banal it is possible to take banality of statement as a statement about banality and hence to derive a suggestion that poetry can go no further than language, which is inevitably distinct from immediate experience, or, alternatively, that poetry should celebrate the objects of the world by simply naming them. The ability of this convention to assimilate anything and endow it with significance may give it a dubious status.[19]

On the other hand there is considerable value in the structuralist emphasis that interpretation of literary work is 'not a matter of recovering some meaning which lies behind the work and serves as a centre governing its structure; it is rather an attempt to participate in and observe the play of possible readings to which the text gives access'.[20]

Harding's account of the relations between 'experience' and 'words' and of the exploratory nature of good poetry provides support for the view that the critic is not concerned to recover some meaning which lies behind the work. However there is a vast amount of verse in which banal thoughts are given banal expression and if the critic dwells on the play or possible readings he may be engaged in the dubious enterprise of endowing 'anything' with significance.

The structuralist rejection of inappropriate models of literature as 'communication' is also of value. Culler rejects 'the tendency to treat a text as if it were spoken and to try to move through the words to recover the meaning which was present in the speaker's mind at the moment of utterance, to determine what the speaker, in that revealing phrase, "had in mind" '.[21] In chapter 7 I will also reject such misleading models of literary 'communication' though I will emphasize, as some structuralists do not, the importance of retaining in criticism a link between a work and its author.

Structuralists' interest in the ways in which a work 'complies with or undermines our procedures for making sense of things' may, as Culler suggests, help to avoid 'premature foreclosure – the unseemly rush from word to world'.

Insisting that literature is something other than a statement about the world, [structuralism] establishes . . . an analogy between the production or reading of signs in literature and in other areas of experience and studies the way in which the former explores and dramatises the latter.

In this kind of interpretation the meaning of a work is what it shows the reader, by the acrobatics in which it involves him, about the problems of his condition as *homo significans*, maker and reader of signs.[22]

Unfortunately it is too often true that acrobatics by the reader, using the text as a springboard for structuralist pyrotechnics, is the consequence of divorcing literature from 'the world'. Sometimes the display is conducted without a text at all – or, rather, with *all* texts. Culler approvingly quotes Barthes' comparison between 'the work' (*any* work) and an onion.

a construction of layers (or levels, or systems) whose body contains, finally no heart, no kernel, no secret, no irreducible principle, nothing except the infinity of its own envelopes – which envelop nothing other than the unity of its own surfaces.[23]

Not to be outdone, Culler elaborates this as follows :

To read is to participate in the play of the text, to locate zones of resistance and transparency, to isolate forms and determine their content and then to treat that content in turn as a form with its own content, to follow, in short, the interplay of surface and envelope.[24]

Matthew Arnold's account of the relation between form and content in the best poetry is subtle, but clear, and it can readily be illustrated. I find Barthes' and Culler's account to be impenetrable and Culler's use of examples to be obscure. He denies that his attempt to 'turn content into form and then to read the significance of the play of forms' reflects a desire to 'fix the text and reduce it to a structure'. Instead, it is 'an attempt to capture its *force*'.[25] This is the first time in Culler's book that we have encountered this concept and these are the final pages. We are offered two illustrations of this key notion, one from Shakespeare and the other from Henry James.

The force, the power of any text, even the most unabashedly mimetic, lies in those moments which exceed our ability to categorize, which collide with our interpretative codes but nevertheless seem right. Lear's 'Pray you, undo this button; thank you, sir' is a gap, a shift in mode which leaves us with two edges and an abyss between them; Milly Theale's 'pink dawn of an apotheosis' before the Bronzino portrait – 'Milly recognized her in words that had nothing to do with her. "I shall never be better than this".' – is one of those interstices where there is a crossing of languages and a sense that the text is escaping us in several directions at once. To define such moments, to speak of their force, would be to identify the codes that encounter resistance there and to delineate the gaps left by a shift in languages.[26]

Some of these phrases seem to me to be apt comment on this as criticism – there is certainly a code here that encounters resistance and collides with my interpretative code. What *are* the two edges and an abyss between them? What *is* an interstice where there is a crossing of languages? How do these comments help us grasp the 'force' of these moments in the texts?

According to Barthes, in learning to cope with literary works the reader becomes 'the hero in the adventures of culture', his pleasure comes from 'the cohabitation of languages which work side by side'.[27] Culler adds that 'the critic, whose job is to display and explain this pleasure, comes to view the text as the happy side of Babel, a set of voices, identifiable or unidentifiable, rubbing against one another and producing both delight and uncertainty'.[28]

This woolly rhapsodizing is insufficiently related to an account of the source of Culler's delight or Barthes' pleasure. Rather, literature becomes the vehicle, or the occasion, for the critic to give fanciful elaboration to his theoretical preoccupations.

Culler might reply that his work might be theoretical, but it's not fanciful. His terminology is closely related to the formidable exponents of deconstructionism in America, particularly those at Yale, a collection of whose work appeared recently as *Deconstruction and Criticism*. There are connections (I could not say they are *clear* connections!) between Culler's words and those of Harold Bloom : 'The breaking of form to produce meaning, as I conceive it, depends upon the operation of certain instances of language, revisionary ratios, and on certain topological displacements in language that intervene between ratios, displacements that I have been calling "crossings".'[29] Bloom offers this as part of an attempt to 'illuminate acts of reading'. A search back through the essay finds no previous reference to 'crossings'. (Do these have something to do with Culler's 'interstices where there is a crossing of languages'?) Bloom's illumination of the act of reading continues by adopting a 'psychic' rather than a 'linguistic' model and he cites the following passage from Anna Freud's *The Ego and the Mechanisms of Defense.*

all the defensive measures of the ego against the id are carried out silently and invisibly. The most that we can ever do is to reconstruct them in retrospect: we can never really witness them in operation. This statement applies, for instance, to successful repression. The ego knows nothing of it: we are aware of it only subsequently when it becomes apparent that something is missing.[30]

Bloom 'applies' this as follows :

As I apply Anna Freud, in a poem the ego is the poetic self and the id is the precursor, idealized and frequently composite, hence fantasized, but still traceable to a historical author or authors. The defensive measures of the poetic self against the fantasized precursor can be witnessed in operation only by the study of a difference between ratios, but this difference depends upon our awareness not so much of presences as of absences, *of what is missing in the poem because it had to be excluded.* It is in this sense that I would grant a point made by John Bayley, that I am 'fascinated by the sort of poetry that is *not really there,* and – even better – the kind that knows it never can be.' But Bayley errs in thinking that this is only one tradition of the poetry of the last three centuries, because clearly it is the norm, or the condition of belated strong poetry. The authentic poem now achieves its dearth of meaning by strategies of exclusion, or what can be called litanies of evasion. I will quote a sympathetic British critic, Roger Poole, for a more useful account of this problematic element in our poetry :

> If a poem is really 'strong' it represents a menace. It menaces the way the reader thinks, loves, fears and is. Consequently, the reading of strong poetry can only take place under conditions of mutual self-defense. Just as the poet must not know what he knows, and must not state what he states, so the reader must not read what he reads. [The] question is not so much 'What does this poem mean?' as 'What has got left out of this poem to make of it the particularly expensive torso that it is?'[31]

Struggling to make any sense at all of this I focus on the word 'expensive'. Is this a misprint for 'expressive'? But that does not help. *How* is the act of reading illuminated by all this? There seems to be some connection between Bloom's and Culler's interest in 'absences' or 'gaps' in literary works and they have a common interest in the 'self-referential' quality of literature. On the other hand deconstructionists are strongly opposed to the structuralist interest in developing a 'science' of literature :

As is abundantly apparent in criticism at the present time, rhetorical analysis, 'semiotics', 'structuralism', 'narratology', or the interpretation of tropes can freeze into a quasi-scientific discipline promising exhaustive rational certainty in the identification of meaning in a text and in the identification of the way that meaning is produced. . . Criticism is a human activity which depends for its validity on never being at ease with a fixed 'method'. It must constantly put its own grounds in question.[32]

This seems to reflect a conception of criticism as a mode of collaborative, questioning, interpretative reasoning of the kind I have offered in previous chapters. Why, then, do deconstructionists retreat from offering their readings of literary works and claim that all that is possible for the critic are 'misreadings' (either 'strong' or 'weak') which are themselves 'texts' which must in turn be 'deconstructed'? There seem to me to be (at least) two possible explanations for this.

(a)   That deconstructionists fail to see the sense in which objectivity of judgement need not imply absolutism or totalitarianism (a distinction for which I argued at length in the previous chapter).

(b)   That they detect absolutism or totalitarianism where it need not exist.

These mistakes are closely connected and they both appear in Professor Hillis Miller's conclusion to *Deconstruction and Criticism*.

> The ultimate justification for this mode of criticism [deconstructionism], as of any conceivable mode, is that it works. It reveals hitherto unidentified meanings and ways of having meaning in major literary texts. The hypothesis of a possible heterogeneity in literary texts is more flexible, more open to a given work, than the assumption that a good work of literature is necessarily going to be 'organically unified'. The latter presupposition is one of the major factors inhibiting recognition of the possibly self-subversive complexity of meanings in a given work. Moreover, 'deconstruction' finds in the text it interprets the double antithetical patterns it identifies. . . It does not claim them as universal explanatory structures, neither for the text in question nor for literature in general. Deconstruction attempts to resist the totalizing and totalitarian tendencies of criticism. It attempts to resist its own tendencies to come to rest in some sense of mastery over the work. It resists these in the name of an uneasy joy of interpretation, beyond nihilism, always in movement, a going beyond which remains in place.[33]

In previous chapters I offered an account of criticism, derived from the work of a variety of critics, which allows for the heterogeneity of literary texts, which is open to this variety, is highly flexible in its approach and which holds that in good works of literature form is intimately, or 'organically', related to content. This belief was not advanced as one which is used to *justify* particular judgements about literary works – it depends upon discriminations already made among various works of literature. 'The critic displays the meanings of his terms by showing how they discriminate among particular cases.' There is nothing in the account I have offered which need inhibit the 'possibly self-subversive complexity of meaning in a given work' (though it would inhibit the 'discovery' of self-subversive complexity of meaning in a poem such as Shelley's 'The Cloud') and there are no 'universal' or 'totalitarian' tendencies in the account. The deconstructionist refusal to accept that any reading could be ultimately definitive is one that I have fully endorsed.

But I do not think that this refusal necessitates the invention of an elaborate apparatus for deconstructing interpretations in an endless process of self-subversion. In fact such an attempt leads to manifest absurdities. As S. L. Goldberg points out in a review of *Deconstruction and Criticism*, there is no reason, on deconstructionist principles, to worry about whether or not we have grasped their arguments (and, when faced with turgidity of the kind cited above from Harold Bloom's essay, this is, as Goldberg drily remarks, a 'pleasing consequence'!):

a true *übermensch* of misreading would not, on deconstructionist principles, be much bothered whether he understood the book or not. . . The textual Superman would easily uphold 'the law', as Professor Hillis Miller puts it, 'that language is not an instrument or tool in man's hands, a submissive means of thinking . . . [but rather it] thinks man and his "world", including poems, if he will allow it to do so.' In his joy, he would simply laugh at any (as it were) 'intentions' that the (as it were) 'authors' of this text may have had in (as it were) 'mind': and in his strength, he would sweep aside their aporias, deconstruct these paper tigers, knock them back into the inter-textual status they came from, and stride away into the abyss. He wouldn't even care whether language will regularly 'think' the text of a bank-cheque into the (as it were) 'pockets' of the (as it were) 'authors' for them allowing it to 'think' their essays and lectures.[34]

Christopher Ricks makes a connected point in his review of Stanley Fish's *Is there a Text in this Class*?

To put it at its simplest, Fish's theory has no way of dealing with misprints. His book happens to be full of misprints. I acknowledge that I call them misprints only by an act of interpretation: that is, I judge that Fish's enterprise in *Is there a text in this class?*, unlike Joyce's in *Finnegan's Wake*, makes it so unlikely that he intended to call the word 'pleasurably' an 'abverb' that I'd feel bound – if I were his executor and he dead – to change it, to correct it for the next printing. Of course he *could* want the word 'abverb' (as in 'pleasurably'), but I so much doubt it that I would bet on it. In other words, we may legitimately judge that we should here read another word ('adverb'), in the most fundamental sense of what it is we should read. The result of my interpreting it as a misprint would be the emendation of the text of this text, and would be the removal thereafter from interpretability at all of the word 'abverb' once so interpreted. Fish didn't mean 'abverb' and so it doesn't make sense to ask what he meant by it. I'd do the same with other misprints here, all of which *could* be in lively creative relation with other words in their vicinity but all of which I am confident are merely misprints: 'distinterested', which might be distantly disinterested, but isn't; 'defintion', which lacks clear definition; 'ambguity', which has one type of it; 'Ftting together', which doesn't; 'innaccurate', which is so (like an Errata-slip which I once saw, headed 'Erata', and which the hermeneuticist might offer as a meta-Errata-slip); 'exhilirating'; and – best of all – 'paristic on everyday usage', which would do very nicely as meaning 'parasitic on Paris' yet which is probably not a revealing pun but a misprint such as reveals nothing except that Harvard University Press lacks good proof-readers. Nothing except that Fish, like other extremists of interpretation, is committed to an inordinate and unworkable sacrosanctity for the text of any text. His theory forbids him to emend, since there isn't anything which he *could* emend, there being no text independent of interpretation, and all interpretation being, on his explicit and detailed account, perfectly self-fulfilling. 'Interpretation creates intention', so you could not posit an intention outside your interpretation; and since interpretations always work perfectly upon whatever they are given, you can't use intention to emend a misprint.[35]

In chapter 7 I will offer a detailed analysis of the notion of authorial intention and its importance in literary criticism and literary education. Although deconstructionists (and structuralists) are right to reject conceptions of authorial intention which encourage the critic to 'reduce' a work of literature to a form of 'personal communication' I have pointed out that there is a strong tradition of criticism which is alert to this kind of distortion but which avoids the absurdities which result from the complete abandonment of a link between author and 'text'.

Deconstructionist and structuralist criticism can be a corrective to the tendency to oversimplify the connections between literature and life or literature and 'the world'. One of the main themes of this book is that the 'reality' of literature is that of a constructed world and its relations to life and events in the real world are often oblique and elusive, requiring for their elucidation considerable critical delicacy and skill. These critical skills are just as necessary for the structuralist or deconstructionist as they are for anyone else. As Culler acknowledged, 'one starts with notions of the meanings or effects of a poem and tries to identify the structures responsible for those effects'. Whether or not one's notions are adequate can only be determined by critical analysis and not even the most avant-garde of the radicals can escape this. I will conclude by trying to demonstrate this point in relation to a particular poem and a particular avant-garde radical.

Terence Hawkes concludes his book *Structuralism and Semiotics* by asking what sort of criticism will replace the old and discredited liberal 'practical' criticism which was merely an ideological outgrowth of capitalism, prizing those values of a decaying aristocracy which are characteristically revered by a sycophantic middle class.

Certainly Barthes and others are prepared to embrace the *total* implications of the work of art's self-referentiality without any limits imposed by a sense of an ultimate 'objective' or concrete reality beyond itself to which the work must be seen to refer. 'New' New Criticism would thus claim to respond to literature's essential nature in which signifiers are prised utterly free of signifieds, aiming in its no-holds-barred encounter with the text, for a *coherence* and validity of response, not objectivity and truth. The most important feature of this process is that it offers a new role and status to the critic. It makes him a participant in the work he reads. The critic *creates* the finished work by his reading of it, and does not remain simply the inert *consumer* of a 'ready-made' product. Thus the critic need not humbly efface himself before the work and submit to its demands: on the contrary, he actively constructs its meaning: he makes the work exist; 'there is no Racine *en soi*. . . Racine exists in the readings of Racine, and apart from the readings there is no Racine.' None of these readings is *wrong*, they all add to the work. So, a work of literature ultimately consists of *everything* that has been said about it.[36]

I want to juxtapose these claims with the account which Hawkes offers of the following poem by William Carlos Williams.

> This is Just to Say
> I have eaten
> the plums
> that were in
> the icebox
> and which
> you were probably
> saving
> for breakfast.
> Forgive me
> they were delicious
> so sweet
> so cold.

In William Carlos Williams' poem . . . the imposition of a new and disturbing status on what would otherwise remain a banal domestic piece of writing is brought about by the visual *iconic* message which says 'this passage of writing constitutes a poem': that is, 'these words have a significance beyond their overt meaning'. Meanwhile, the *symbolic* signs emitted lack any of the indications of 'poemness' that our culture leads us to look for and expect. By these means, the poem is able to make us think about what those expectations really are and whether or not we really endorse them. It even makes us think about the nature of the social conventions which invest 'poems' with 'significance', but deny it to other forms of utterance. In thus using *iconic* means to subvert our expectations [the poem] proves fundamentally disturbing. [Footnote] Compare Culler's interesting discussion of Williams' poem [the text of which is cited in note 37]. It will be clear that although I agree that 'when it is set down on the page as a poem the convention of significance comes into play', I do not accept Culler's conclusion that 'we must therefore supply a new function to justify the poem.' The poem's 'justification' seems to me to reside in its implicit questioning of the 'convention of significance.' It is about its own status and the social processes that determine our response to its language.[38]

In view of Hawkes' claims for 'New' New Criticism this dispute has a rather old-fashioned ring to it. Surely Hawkes is denying Culler's right to 'create the finished work by his reading of it'. How can Hawkes refuse to accept Culler's justification for the poem when no reading of the poem is wrong, when all readings add to the work? It would appear that Culler has failed to 'embrace the *total* implications of the work of art's self-referentiality' and has 'imposed limits by a sense of an ultimate "objective" or concrete reality beyond itself to which the work [is] seen to refer'. Culler's mistake is to think that a poem might be about something else than itself and he has missed the opportunity for a no-holds-barred encounter with the text by failing to prise signifiers utterly free of signifieds. But how can Hawkes show Culler the error of his ways except by engaging in old-fashioned practical criticism?

As it happens I think that Hawkes' account is a more adequate analysis of what Williams' poem is doing than is Culler's, though the poem is by no means 'disturbing' and is much more a 'jeu' than a commentary on the 'social processes that determine our response to its language'. But if this is too weighty for the poem to support, Culler's interpretation crushes it completely. Even if we were to grant that the last few lines of the poem affirm 'the value of immediate sensuous experience', I cannot see why this is something that 'transcends language and cannot be captured by the poem except negatively (as apparent insignificance) which is why the poem must be so sparse and superficially banal'. The value of immediate sensuous experience is often very powerfully realized in poetry.

I am unable, as well, to accept the suggestion the poem is offering that the order of personal relationships (the relationships between the 'I' and the 'you' in the poem) must make a place for such sensuous reference. There is too little substance in the poem to justify the claim that it evokes a relationship, but in so far as it does, the final three lines surely suggest that the relationship between the 'you' and the 'I' is one in which the pleasure the 'I' receives from eating the plums is something that the 'you' will welcome rather than resent. There is no need to 'make a place for sensuous experience' between them and no need for forgiveness.

I think the poem gestures towards a 'content' that Hawkes ignores and which Culler overstates and misinterprets. It coyly suggests a degree of intimate mutuality and domesticity. And there is an attempt at dramatic effectiveness in presenting the reader with a domestic note in the form of a poem. The reader is addressed by the note as if he were the 'you' and is obliged to respond to it as if it were an actual communication, not merely between the 'I' and the 'you' in the poem but between the 'I' and oneself. This obliges us to imagine what response the 'I' expects from the recipient to the last three lines.

But neither Hawkes' nor Culler's (nor my own) case rescues the poem from banality. Culler's *instinct* is right to look for some 'further justification' for the poem than its questioning 'the convention of significance'. Hawkes gives us no reason why *any* transcription of prose into verse, no matter how banal, might not do as well as Williams' example. So although Hawkes is right to think that Culler's attempted 'justification' is misguided, Hawkes' contention that the poem is 'fundamentally disturbing' is entirely unsupported. No *critical* argument is advanced for this and only such argument could 'rescue' the poem.

Neither deconstructionism nor structuralism offers an *alternative* to criticism of the kind I have outlined in earlier chapters. If, as Hillis Miller claims of deconstructionism, the ultimate justification for this or any other mode of criticism is that it 'works' – 'It reveals hitherto unidentified meanings and ways of having meaning in major literary texts' – then the test of the value of these or any other literary theories is through the comparative analysis of particular works of literature.

David Lodge has referred to a 'pendulum of fashion'[39] in twentieth-century literature and criticism, between 'realism' and 'modernism', 'life' and 'art', 'didacticism' and 'aestheticism', 'content' and 'form'. I argued earlier that any criticism which emphasizes 'form' at the expense of 'content', or 'content' at the expense of 'form', will fail to do justice to the distinctive ways in which literary works reflect on (play with/entertain) human life and its concerns (including, of course, the 'self-reflexive' concerns of the artist). Lodge's explorations of the 'ontology and typology of literature'[40] employ some structuralist ideas, particularly those of Jakobson, in order to try to contain or override the swings of the pendulum of fashion. But there is nothing distinctively structuralist about Lodge's essays on Hardy's novels in his most recent book.[41] Lodge's starting point for his approach to the novel is precisely that which I adopted in chapter 2. 'In the form of a novel, all the components are interdependent. Its effect is cumulative and every word makes its contribution.'[42] Lodge offers a critical account of *Jude the Obscure* in which he draws our attention to 'the way the form of *Jude* works to articulate and reinforce the pessimism of its vision of life'.

I use the word *form* in its widest sense to include all the means of literary presentation; from the largest to the smallest in scope: the design of the plot, the point of view of the narrator, symbolic action, figurative language, right down to the construction of the simplest sentences. In one sense everything in a novel is form, since it is only by virtue of having form that a novel communicates at all.[43]

Criticism which is informed by this awareness of the ways in which 'parts relate to parts and they to whole' in good literature is, of course, criticism of the kind for which I argued earlier. I would argue as well that the best corrective to the swings of critical fashion is the practice and teaching of such criticism.

At another point in his book *Working with Structuralism*, Lodge discusses criticism in which the 'underlying aim was to demonstrate that what looked like redundant or random detail in realistic fiction was in fact functional, contributing to a pattern of motifs with expressive and thematic significance'. He comments that the practitioners of such criticism were unaware that Roman Jakobson had 'provided a theoretical justification for this kind of criticism in his famous definition of literariness, or the poetic function of language, as "the projection of the principle of equivalence from the axis of selection to the axis of combination" '.[44]

To reject this 'justification' is not necessarily to join those academics who, according to Lodge, 'convinced themselves that if they kept their heads down long enough the whole structuralist fuss will blow over'. Any general principles or definitions of 'literariness' have significance only in so far as the criticism to which they are related 'works'. Not only do they not justify the criticism, such principles and definitions could not, as I argued in the previous chapter, be clearly understood, 'unless one had a prior grasp of the concrete judgements they were supposed to justify'.

5

Literature and the education of the emotions

(a) 'Cognitive' and 'affective' objectives in literary education: a false dichotomy

It is commonly claimed by literary theorists, and sometimes by teachers, that reading works of literature educates the emotions. In fact literary education is often held to be concerned with emotional development, while science, mathematics and so on are held to be concerned with the development of understanding.

I pointed out earlier that there is widespread dissatisfaction among English teachers with the teaching of literary criticism. This dissatisfaction with what W. A. Murray calls the 'sterile cant' that many English students become practised in for examination purposes often leads to a thorough-going rejection of a literary critical approach to literature in education as being merely 'cognitive'. This is accompanied by an insistence that it is the 'experience' of literature which is important in order to promote 'the education of the emotions'. The following extract from a recent essay on the teaching of literature is representative of the views of many English teachers.

It is a fact that *cognitive* discourses occupy almost the entire secondary school curriculum. Affective discourses (the arts) get scant recognition on the timetable. The imbalance is both huge and frightening. It is, therefore, a tragic irony that literature, which has as its object the education of the emotions, should be perverted by examinations into a predominantly cognitive mode. To stop examining literature would be to remove from large numbers of pupils the *only* affective discourse they are exposed to at school. To examine it by present methods is to subordinate what really matters, the *experience* of literature, to abstract, critical talk *about* literature.[1]

In previous chapters I acknowledged the potentially 'perverting' influence of examinations on the teaching of literature, the way in which they encourage an approach to the teaching of literary criticism which is stereotyped, formulaic and sterile. There is a danger that the consequence of disillusion with the methods of assessment and teaching will be a thorough-going rejection of literary criticism in education and some serious misconceptions about the 'aims' of literary education. The account I have offered of literary criticism attempts to establish that far from being external talk 'about' literature, literary criticism is the articulation of our total response to literary works, a response in which thought and feeling (or 'cognitive' and 'affective' elements) are inseparably related or part of one another.

In the argument to follow I want to establish that a disjunction between 'cognitive' and 'affective' objectives in education is logically incoherent and that it is unintelligible to advance 'the education of the emotions' as an aim which could be independent of cognitive development. I will begin by attacking one of the main sources of the divorce between cognitive and affective objectives in education, the work of B. S. Bloom and his colleagues.[2] Bloom's work has had enormous influence – in an article about the teaching of English, George Allen acknowledges that Bloom's taxonomies of educational objectives have become perhaps 'the single strongest influence upon contemporary thinking about the curriculum in the English-speaking world'.[3]

Bloom inclines strongly towards the view that teaching values is indoctrination, and he suggests that we leave it up to individual students to work out their own personal 'likes' or 'dislikes', 'attitudes', 'commitments' and 'preferences' about values.

Cognitive behaviour may be used to indoctrinate points of view and to build up attitudes and values. Indeed we do this shamelessly in the aesthetic fields, where we want our students to recognize 'good' poetry, painting, architecture, sculpture, music and so on. But in most areas of the curriculum we have a horror of indoctrinating the students with any but our most basic core values (we cannot always agree on the nature of these core values, the court cases on religion in the schools are an example). In most instances where indoctrination is avoided we seek to have the student take his own position with respect to the issue. Thus a discussion may result in a variety of 'correct' positions and attitudes with respect to the area of concern, rather than a single type of behavioural outcome as where a cognitive objective has been achieved. This also occurs where there are conflicts in values within our own culture. For example, the problems of honesty vs dishonesty vs 'white lies' or of competition vs cooperation usually result in a variety of acceptable solutions, each a function of the situation in which such conflict arises.[4]

The achievement of a 'cognitive' objective in education has a single outcome because Bloom largely accepts that there are 'right' or 'wrong' answers in areas such as science, whereas, since no one in Bloom's view can claim to be right or wrong about moral or aesthetic beliefs, indoctrination is to be avoided by letting 'attitudes', 'appreciations', 'commitments' in these areas develop according to the individual's own preferences (except with regard to our 'most basic core values' !).

In chapter 3 I argued that while there may be more widespread agreement in some areas of science than there is in some areas of literary criticism this need not constitute a threat to the possibility of objectivity in criticism. It does not occur to Bloom that any case could be made out for the possibility of objectivity in the moral and aesthetic domains. In fact, in the passage just cited, he implicitly denies that these are even 'cognitive' areas, a position which seems close to the positivist view so vividly expressed by Carnap : 'Many linguistic utterances are analogous to laughing in that they have only an expressive function, no representative function. Examples of these are cries like 'Oh, oh', or, on a higher level, lyrical verses.'[5] Bloom separates the area of moral and aesthetic attitudes, appreciations, preferences, commitments and so on into a separate domain, 'the affective domain'. Since this solution to the problem of fitting the teaching of values into educational objectives by treating values as matters of personal 'opinion' or subjective 'feeling' is a popular one, I will give Bloom's work a detailed scrutiny.

In *Handbook I, The Cognitive Domain*, Bloom tacitly assumes that education is concerned with the development of mind through knowledge and that falsehood and indoctrination are to be avoided. It is because he makes this tacit assumption that he makes no reference to such possible objectives as 'getting children to use alchemical techniques in effecting changes in metals' or 'analysing personality characteristics by using phrenology' or 'predicting future events astrologically'. The taxonomy reflects the assumptions of the teachers whose views are 'taxonomised' that 'cognitive objectives' in education are tied to knowledge and objectivity. Astrological and alchemical procedures cannot be included among the forms of analysis and synthesis to be developed in education because astrology and alchemy are not forms of knowledge.

In *Handbook II, The Affective Domain*, however, the domain

of affective objectives in education is separated from knowledge
and objectivity, with disastrous consequences. We can no longer
assume, in *Handbook II*, that 'affective objectives' such as 'satisfaction in response' or 'commitment' relate to the development of
desirable states of mind. I have just pointed out that, in the cognitive domain, the guarantee that the skills and abilities are educationally desirable is provided by the dependence of such skills as
'analysis' and 'synthesis' on the standards and procedures for
establishing knowledge and objectivity of judgement in the various
forms of knowledge. So that although Bloom claims in the first
handbook that every effort was made to avoid value judgements
about objectives and behaviours, to 'permit the inclusion of objectives from all educational orientations', the decision to discriminate
educational objectives is associated with a fundamental value
judgement – that education is concerned with the development
of mind through knowledge or objective judgement. *Handbook I*
assumes tacitly that indoctrination, bias and falsehood are to be
avoided. In the second handbook, however, 'affective objectives'
in education are described as if they were separable from the
development of knowledge and objective judgement and the illustrative test items reinforce this impression. When we ask, of the
objectives offered, 'satisfaction in response to what?' or 'commitment to what?' the answers we are given through the examples in
the test items do not refer us to standards of what is true, or 'objectively' good or right, presumably because Bloom sees it as his task
to be 'neutral' with respect to 'value questions'.

When Bloom explains the 'neutrality' of the taxonomy he says
that what is meant is that it 'should be broad enough to include
objectives from any philosophic orientation and thus from any
culture'.

> It seems unlikely that the publicly avowed objectives of most schools, in
> western society, would differ markedly from ours in America even when
> the political orientation is markedly more authoritarian. On the other
> hand, the scheme does provide levels for the inculcation of a prescribed
> set of values if this is the philosophy of a culture.[6]

Two points become apparent here :

(a) The taxonomy is referred to as a classification of 'school'
objectives; the distinction between these and educational
objectives is ignored.

(b)   The consequences of a failure to observe this distinction are apparent in the second sentence where Bloom's 'neutrality' leads him to accept what appears to be a form of indoctrination as embodying objectives for which the taxonomy ought to make room. This would be inappropriate in a taxonomy of *educational* objectives. While there will be wide differences as to whether a particular set of beliefs does constitute a 'doctrine', the extreme 'inculcation of a prescribed set of values' exhibits a lack of concern for whether the values are defensible or not. Without such a concern we would be unable to distinguish education from indoctrination.[7]

In the first handbook Bloom tells us that 'We recognize the point of view that truth and knowledge are only relative and that there are no hard and fast truths which exist for all time and all places.' As I have explained, there was no need to challenge the epistemological assumptions which are implied by this remark. For this 'recognition' does not lead Bloom to allow the passing on of false beliefs and specious procedures as legitimate educational objectives, at least in the first handbook. Bloom is not 'neutral' with regard to knowledge and truth. His view that they are 'relative' does not lead him to make room, in *The Cognitive Domain*, for the development of false beliefs and specious procedures if *these* are part of the 'philosophy of a culture'. But no restrictions are placed, even tacitly, on the 'values' which may be passed on in education. I shall argue that this crucial divorce between the two domains (which are logically indivisible) is disastrous for the second handbook.

Bloom acknowledges frequently enough that 'at all levels of the affective domain, affective objectives have a cognitive component', but he fails to see that this cognitive component (the 'judgement' or 'the way someone "sees" the object of feeling') is the crucial factor in determining whether an affective response is desirable or not and thus whether it is an appropriate educational objective. Education may be distinguished from other processes such as indoctrination because the judgements and evaluations which children are taught to make can be seen to relate to the acceptable procedures or criteria for making judgements and evaluations in the various forms of knowledge and objective judgement. I am arguing that the criteria for making evaluations (in morals or literary criticism or whatever) are the only criteria for estimating the desirability of an affective response in such areas and thus for determining whether or not a particular affective objective is an educational objective. The business of education in the affective domain is to get students to feel positively towards what is valuable or true or right in so far as there are acceptable criteria for determining truth or goodness or rightness. Those criteria are not contingently related to the specification of educational objectives in the affective domain – they are a necessary part of such a specification.

My defence in chapter 3 of the possibility of objectivity in aesthetic judgements was not intended to deny the point that the criteria in this area are often obscure and contested. Bloom notes this when he refers to the objective 'responds emotionally to a work of art'. He remarks, 'While we could recognize a cognitive component in such an objective we should clearly be less certain to secure agreement among educators about the most appropriate cognitive behaviour to accompany the affective behaviour.'[8] But the difficulty here, and throughout most of the second handbook, is at least partly of Bloom's own making. For 'responds emotionally to a work of art' should never have been admitted as an educational objective. If the objective were to be properly stated it would read, 'responds with an appropriate emotion to particular works of art'.[9] Affective responses such as this require for their elucidation very close attention to the way a student *sees* a particular work of art. This 'cognitive' behaviour does not merely 'accompany' the affective behaviour – it is an essential part of the analysis of the affective behaviour.

C. A. Mace sums up a conclusion which is common to preceding philosophical discussions of 'emotions' which can be extended to all 'affective' responses : 'Every emotional or affective state involves a "judgement", an appraisal of a situation, a perception of some feature of the situation, some kind of cognition.'[10] But, Mace adds, the 'cognitive' component can take the form of a grossly mistaken belief. Similarly, Peters argues that the 'standard uses' of 'emotion' and other affective terms refer to something which 'comes over people when they consider a situation in a certain kind of light' – and this consideration frequently involves a misapprehension of the situation or phenomenon.

This point is important when we consider what is involved in achieving educational objectives in the so-called affective domain. In the analysis of a student's affective response to a work of art, for example, it is crucial to get at the way the child sees the work. The only way we can get him to feel differently about it is to get him to see it differently. And the only way we can decide whether or not the student's response is appropriate or inappropriate is by referring to whatever criteria are available for making judgements about works in the particular art form.

It does occur to Bloom on one occasion that the 'cognitive' analysis of a work of art may be necessary for 'truly' appreciating a work of art.

> In some instances teachers use cognitive behaviour not just as a means to affective behaviour but as a kind of prerequisite. Thus appreciation objectives are often approached cognitively by having the student analyse a work of art so that he will come to understand the way in which certain effects are produced – the nuances of shading to produce depth, colour to produce emotional tone, etc. Such analysis on a cognitive level, when mastered, may be seen as learning necessary for 'truly' appreciating a work of art.[11]

This is not the place to embark on a full-scale analysis of the concept of appreciation[12] but we must observe that Bloom fails to see the sense in which an appropriate cognitive core to the 'appreciation' *is* necessary. In so far as the student is responding to irrelevant features of the work then he is not truly appreciating the work. It is of no consequence that he may have great difficulty in articulating the reasons for his response. For example, confronted with Turner's painting *The Slave Ship* he may only be able to say, 'It's something to do with the light in the painting that I appreciate most.' Such an appreciation must be distinguished from another which is 'appreciative' because the painting is 'in a nice frame' or because 'It's so big.' In *every* case, of course, the affective response relates to 'a perception of some feature of the situation, some kind of cognition'. It would be educationally uninformative if the students just said that they 'liked' the painting. The achievement of educational objectives in the affective domain is necessarily related to the cognitive core of the affective responses, to the appropriateness of the way the object of the affective response is perceived. Bloom notes that there may be a variety of 'correct' responses. But he nowhere emphasizes the corollary of this – that it is often possible to distinguish between 'correct' and 'incorrect' responses.

Bloom distinguishes sharply between 'evaluation' which he offers as a 'cognitive' objective and 'appreciation' which is offered as an 'affective' objective. He cites the following as a test of a student's capacity for 'evaluation' :

Given a poem, determine criteria of evaluation which are appropriate and apply them.

> Since there's no help, come let us kiss and part;
> Nay I have done, you get no more of me,
> And I am glad, yea glad with all my heart
> That thus so clearly I myself can free;
> Shake hands forever, cancel all our vows,
> And when we meet at any time again,
> Be it not seen in either of our brows
> That we one jot of former love retain.
> Now at the last gasp of love's latest breath,
> When, his pulse failing, passion speechless lies,
> When faith is kneeling by his bed of death,
> And innocence is closing up his eyes,
> Now if thou wouldst, when all have given him over,
> From death to life thou mightst him yet recover.

Write an essay of from 250–500 words, describing and evaluating the foregoing poem. In your description you should employ such terms as will reveal your recognition of formal characteristics of the poem. Your principles of evaluation should be made clear – although they should not be elaborately described or defended.[13]

Bloom rightly takes it for granted that 'truly evaluating' this poem requires the exercise of a number of cognitive skills. But he is not willing to assume that 'truly *appreciating*' a poem will also require 'critical' skills. Unless someone were able to identify the roguish persuasion of the last lines, for example, we would have to deny that he had truly appreciated the poem. Part of what is *meant* by 'appreciating' a poem is that the reader is responding to those aspects of the poem which make it a good poem and this is part of what is involved in evaluation of the poem. In this sense, 'evaluation', with all the cognitive operations it may involve, is a logically necessary part of what constitutes an educational objective in the affective domain of literary studies. As Leavis puts it, 'The critic's aim is, first, to realize as sensitively as possible this or that which claims his attention; and a certain valuing is implicit in the realizing.'[14]

(b) Emotions in literature and emotions in life

I have maintained that the appropriateness or otherwise of our emotional responses to works of literature is dependent upon the adequacy of our understanding of the works. But what connections are there between the emotions which are appropriate to seeing a performance of *King Lear* or reading *Anna Karenina* and those which are a consequence of our involvement with people and events in the real world? In the context of the alleged 'education of the emotions' through literature this is obviously a fundamental question. Teachers usually expect their students to be 'moved' by what they read; but what is the relation between the emotions we feel as we 'participate in' or 'enter into' a novel, play or poem and the emotions we feel in the context of everyday life?

I have argued that all emotions are differentiated in relation to one's perception of objects or circumstances. The perception we have of the objects or circumstances portrayed in works of literature is, usually, of fictional objects or circumstances. If we become 'caught up' in the world of a book or a play we rarely lose sight of the fact that it is a book or a play. (Though I will shortly consider some occasions when, apparently, we do momentarily lose sight of this fact.)

This is not to say that the emotions experienced in relation to a book or a play are less 'real' or less profound than those we experience in actual life. It is only to say that the reality or profundity of the emotions we experience in response to literary works is occasioned by the perception of a presented or constructed 'world'. It is part of the 'cognitive core' of our emotional response to a book or a play that what we are perceiving is not real. As Susanne Langer argues,

Virtual life, as good literature presents it, is always a self-contained form, a unit of experience, in which every element is related organically to every other element, no matter how capricious or fragmentary the items are made to appear. That very caprice or fragmentation is a total *effect*, which requires a perception of the whole history as a fabric of contributive events.[15]

However, when Langer denies that literature is, as a consequence, less 'vivid' than life, she says, 'We sometimes praise a novel for approaching the vividness of events; usually however it exceeds them in vividness.' I think that this is misleading since the vividness of events and people in actual life may not be straightforwardly compared with the vividness of 'events' and 'people' in a constructed world. What sense can be made of the suggestion that Wordsworth's daffodils are more vivid than the daffodils in that field over there, or that King Lear is more vivid than my grandfather, or that Dickens' descriptions of life in nineteenth-century England are more vivid than the life that was actually led? This is an unusual lapse for Langer, since she manages so firmly to specify the fundamental *distinctness* of actuality from representations or portrayals in art. Nevertheless it is important to emphasize the error since it is closely related to some prevailing misconceptions about the connection between literary emotions and non-literary emotions.

I use these terms deliberately since much ink has been spilled in philosophy journals attempting to decide whether or not the emotions we experience in relation to literary works are 'real' emotions. But it is misleading to ask, 'How can we experience real emotions in response to events and people we know are not real?', since the question involves some false assumptions about what constitutes a real emotion. The emotions we experience in response to the representations or portrayals of events and characters in literary works are not less *real* because they have, as their objects, representations or portrayals of characters and events. As H. O. Mounce points out, 'It is evident that there are things in life that move us. This being so, why on earth should it be surprising that we should be moved by representations of such things? Would it not be more surprising if we were not so moved?'[16] However, Mounce goes on to argue that the verisimilitude of literary and dramatic representations may be so exact, 'so very like the real thing as to produce what in most respects is the same emotion'. The example he offers is of a vivid and realistic film portrayal of the gouging out of Gloucester's eyes.

At first glance this seems to be related to the point that Langer makes (and to which I objected) that events in a novel may be as (or more) vivid than actual events. But Mounce's example suggests that he has something much more limited and specific in mind than Langer. In the cinema the illusion of reality may be so powerful that we may feel emotions in response to the portrayal of events which are more or less indistinguishable from those that we would feel towards actual events. There are two points I want to make about this.

1. This powerful illusion of reality in the cinema is a momentary one. In the film of *King Lear* it is the momentary horror that overcomes us as (presumably) we see Gloucester's eyeballs being forced out of their sockets (by means of what are called 'special effects'). We recoil more or less as we would in reaction to seeing an actual occurrence of eye-gouging partly because it is realistically presented and partly because the realistic details are unexpected. The techniques are familiar in horror movies – we are 'caught off guard' – the monster suddenly appears before our eyes and the audience screams. And then there's the ripple of relief as everyone settles back in their seats, savouring the shock as they return to reality. The reality, of course, is that they are safely watching a movie, a portrayal of events. (It is significant too that if we see the film again we are not likely to be 'caught off guard' again. It seems most unlikely that one observation of actual eye-gouging would make us less vulnerable to the next.)

2. It is always relevant to ask whether or not such realistic effects in the filming of a play or novel are part of and contribute to an adequate understanding and appreciation of the work. When Gloucester's eyes are being removed all kinds of things are taking place, and if our preoccupation with 'sensational' images blurs or distorts our perception of the interaction of the characters involved the *significance* of the event in the play could be lost. The gouging is plainly evocative of horror and repulsion ('Out, vile jelly') but to show us details of gushing blood, eyeballs and empty sockets seems more likely to produce, merely for its own sake, a primitive reaction to an image.

Mounce maintains that 'The roots of art are the same as those of magic. They lie in our primitive reactions to images.'[17] Consequently he condemns the 'oversophistication' of other contributors to the debate, such as Michael Weston,[18] who argues that our emotional involvement in an event or with a character in a play or novel is not separable from our perception of the other aspects of the work with which the characters and events are in interaction, and which define or 'place' their significance. I have maintained that a strong case can be made out for what D. H. Lawrence called the 'subtle interrelatedness' of good literature. Weston is clearly not referring to thrillers or tear-jerkers or horror movies in which the *whole point* is merely to trigger off horror or sadness or fear in the viewer or reader. Since the development of the cinema it is easy to contrive an 'illusion of reality' and any director can provide us with images to which we will react primitively. But such reactions are reactions to conjuring or illusion-making and may have no association with art at all.

Of course it is *possible* that the director of the film of *King Lear* would do a good job; perhaps his 'special effects' *would* contribute to the dramatic enactment or 'realization' of the play. I introduce the literary critical terms deliberately because the term 'realization', as it is employed by a critic such as Leavis, cannot be reduced to 'making real' in the sense of providing verisimilitude (or 'illusions of reality') as an end in itself. No literary or dramatic talent is necessary to achieve such an end, one only needs a few tricks. Such elementary skill may sometimes be exercised by a serious artist in the course of controlling and orchestrating the varying degrees of emotional engagement we have in the action or pattern of events he presents. In a major film, such as Hitchcock's *Psycho*, our emotional engagement or disengagement in events, or with particular characters, is directed with great subtlety towards profoundly serious artistic ends. In this respect the film critic Robin Wood has argued convincingly that Hitchcock's films sometimes share some of the qualities and concerns of Shakespeare's plays.[19] Of course Hitchcock was, as the cliché goes, also 'the master of suspense' and as part of the complex 'realization' of his major films he made the most effective use of 'primitive reactions to images'. But in his best films[20] the 'heart-stopping moment' is never employed for its own sake. It forms part of the whole orchestrated 'flow and recoil of sympathy' to which D. H. Lawrence refers (in the context of the novelist's art).

Mounce rejects, as 'oversophisticated', attempts to argue that there are significant differences between being moved by tear-jerkers and sob-stories and being moved by novels such as *Anna Karenina*. He denies that it makes any difference that our emotional reaction to Anna's fate is bound up with, is inseparable from, the whole complex of feelings, thoughts, incidents and characters that comprise the novel. He claims that any attempt to distinguish between the emotions generated by 'great art' and those produced by a sob-story is beside the point : 'The problem is that of understanding how anyone can be moved by a fiction of whatever kind.'[21] But this is in direct conflict with the point that Mounce has already made, that there is no problem here at all ('why on earth should it be surprising ... ?'). This is a philosopher's pseudo problem, as Mounce himself has effectively demonstrated.

Mounce retains respect for the 'unsophisticate who sobs at Hollywood slush', claiming that 'the response is at least genuine', and he implies that the 'sophisticate' who registers a complex response to Anna Karenina's fate is merely treating her as an element in a complex game. He ignores Weston's argument that 'the interpretation of a work of art is not a self contained game, but has its importance in connection with what is not art, with our everyday lives'. 'If we are moved through the significance we see an event possesses within the thematic context of a play, that such significance should matter to us is not itself explained by the play but must be accounted for by the way literature can illuminate our lives.'[22] I do not want to underestimate the complexity of the connections between literature and life; nor do I want to promote what David Holbrook calls 'the new aestheticism – a split between art and life'. Holbrook wants the literature student to 'accept or reject' literary experience by 'testing it against his own experience'. Unless students do so, according to Holbrook, literature will not 'mean anything that bears on their own experience or attitudes to life – it is "apart" as "literature" '.[23] But how, for example, do we test the experience of reading *Anna Karenina* against our own experience? If we focus on the presentation of Anna's experience we might, for example, try to test Anna's decision to leave her husband and child against our own experience. Quite apart from the questions which immediately arise about the *adequacy* of our own experience, there are questions concerning the relationship between Anna's experience and the ways in which all the other characters in the novel deal with the conflicting forces and values of hedonism, despair, selfishness, deceit, fidelity, passion and, most importantly, love, as these are experienced in the (presented) lives of all the characters. Anna's experience (or our experience of Anna) is *part* of the experience of this complex whole. We cannot *isolate* her experience and test it against our own because her experience is a constitutive part of the entire imaginative exploration of life that makes up the novel. We can *only* test her experience against our own if we are able to hold it in tension with other (presented) experiences that enter into the novel. This is an undertaking which makes considerable demands on the reader's critical capacities.

In the course of a literary education designed to develop such critical capacities it may frequently happen that the student's capacity for genuine response becomes atrophied and the criticism degenerates into sterile game-playing. This, apparently, is Mounce's concern. But a genuine response to Anna Karenina cannot be independent of a genuine response to *Anna Karenina*, and that is not to treat her as an element in a complex game. It is complex, certainly, but it is not a game, so long as the genuineness of the response is not lost in oversophistication. And ensuring this is a personal or a pedagogical problem, not a philosophical problem.

(c) Literature as an alternative to life

In section (a) of this chapter I tried to establish that if literary education is concerned to develop the adequacy and appropriateness of students' emotional responses to literary works then this necessarily entails the development of the adequacy and appropriateness of their perceptions of literary works. That is to say that 'the education of the emotions' through literature is dependent upon some form of literary critical education, since literary criticism is centrally concerned with the adequacy and appropriateness of the ways in which we perceive works of literature.

There are some English teachers and literary theorists who, while they might concede this point, would feel that I had missed the most important aspect of the education of the emotions through literature. They would suggest that it is not merely the development of finer and more appropriate responses *to literary works* that is the significant objective. It is the *general* emotional development and psychic health of the individual that is a primary objective. Writers who emphasize this kind of objective characteristically derive their theoretical assumptions from psychology and psychoanalytic theory. For example, most of the authors cited in the 'theoretical' section of the Schools Council Research Study, *Children and their Books*,[24] are either psychologists or psychoanalysts. They stress, above all, the child's (and the adult's) quest for instinctual satisfaction in his reading, particularly those related to the emotional conflicts and problems which are uppermost at his particular stage of development. Writers in this tradition have tended to speak in terms of empathy, identification and disguised or substitute gratification of unconscious wishes; in general their conclusion has been that a major motive leading children (and adults) to prefer their favourite books is a desire to obtain vicarious imaginative satisfaction of a wish-fulfilment kind, often by means of identification with a hero or heroine not too unlike themselves.[25]

In the next chapter I will examine in more detail the nature of empathy and its importance in literary education. Prior to this more specific issue, however, there is the broader suggestion in the psychological and psychoanalytic work that literature, for its readers, is a kind of emotional substitute for, or alternative to, life. The Schools Council Report cites Simon O. Lesser's account of the role of fiction in human life. Starting with a quotation from Freud ('the meagre satisfaction that man can extract from reality leaves him starving') Lesser lists some of the 'inherent and inescapable deficiencies of real experience' and concludes as follows :

It is to make good some of the deficiencies of experience that people read fiction. ... we read because we are beset by anxieties, guilt feelings and ungratified needs. The reading of fiction permits us in indirect fashion to satisfy those needs, relieve our anxieties and assuage our guilt. It transports us into a realm more comprehensible and coherent, more passionate and plastic, and at the same time more compatible with our ideals than the world of daily routine, thus providing a kind of experience which is qualitatively superior to that which we ordinarily obtain from life.[26]

One objection to this is that it is absurdly sweeping. Different people read different things at different times for different reasons. Sometimes we may read a book to try to make up for the in-adequacy of life; but do we really satisfy our ungratified needs, relieve our anxieties or assuage our guilt by reading books? (What does Lesser have in his library ? !) The Schools Council authors are particularly concerned with another obvious objection to Lesser's suggestion that literature is an escapist substitute for life, which is that much fiction includes 'the presentation of experiences which are unpleasurable, painful, even deeply distressing'. Their concern is due to the fact that they want to 're-instate wish-fulfilment accomplished by means of identification to a position quite near the centre of the fiction-reading process'. In order to defend 'the pleasure principle' as the 'dominant motivation of the reader of fiction' they offer several answers to the 'problem' created by fiction which presents painful or distressing experiences.

Their first suggestion is fairly unobjectionable – often the unpleasurable episodes 'prepare for, heighten or enhance a subsequent wish-fulfilment gratification' in the course of our reading a story. But the phrase 'wish-fulfilment gratification' has a very portentous ring to it and, as the second suggestion in defence of 'the pleasure principle' is developed, this pseudo-psychologizing gets quite out of hand. The Schools Council authors argue that 'one function of the unpleasurable element in fiction is to disguise from consciousness the fact that wish-fulfilment gratifications are being attained, particularly in cases where the wish in question has been repressed or has guilt feelings attached to it'.[27]

Consider, in the light of this, the reader of *Anna Karenina*. His response to Anna's suffering and eventual suicide has the function of disguising from his consciousness the repressed and guilty wish-fulfilment gratifications he has attained from vicariously enjoying Anna's passionate and illicit love affair. This is both a falsification of the complex emotional structure of the novel and an untestable diagnosis of the reader's response. Who is to know, how could it be demonstrated, that the *real* source of anyone's interest in the novel is 'pleasure' and that the painful and distressing episodes enable us to 'cover up with a disguise our instinctual gratifications'? Are those readers who deny this in need of psychoanalysis in order to expose the ways in which they have merely been disguising their guilt feelings about the unconscious 'instinctual' pleasure they have received from their reading? The Schools Council authors apparently believe so, as may be seen in this passage :

it may be suggested that as we move towards the more serious and the more complexly structured end of the fictional continuum [referred to earlier as 'great literature'] we shall meet works in which the underlying wishes are both more deeply rooted in the human psyche and more strongly repressed by the conscious personality, and in which as a corollary the satisfaction of these wishes is more elaborately disguised by a realism which accords due weight to the unpleasant or distressing aspects of human experience.[28]

In order to defend 'the pleasure principle' as the dominant motivation for the reading of fiction we are offered this facile psychologizing, which does not begin to do justice to our response to 'serious'
and 'complexly structured' works of literature such as *Anna
Karenina*. However, the Schools Council authors themselves
appear unconvinced by their own argument:

It must be said that there are also occasions when the painful element
seems to be present more for its own sake than as a foil to something
else. As an example, one might point to moments in *Jane Eyre* which
seem to involve a masochistic enjoyment, on the part of the reader, of
imagined experiences of persecution, humiliation or subjection to in-
justice.[29]

Fortunately, it is unnecessary to re-iterate and develop my objections to the pseudo-psychologizing that follows about 'the complex
phenomenon of masochism' because not even this satisfies the
authors that they have transmuted all apparently unpleasurable
literary experiences into pleasurable ones:

Even so, it may be asked whether there are not still some instances of a
painful or disturbing experience in fiction which are more properly
thought of as manifestations of the reality principle and which it would
be more natural to approach in terms of Harding's view of fiction as
'a convention for enlarging the discussions we have with each other
about what might befall'.[30]

We are now told that 'the reader's spectator role' may include 'the
realistic acceptance of unwelcome and unwished for aspects of
human experience'. Why, then, have the Schools Council authors
invested so much energy in trying to explain this away? Why is it
argued at this point that what needs stressing is that '*in most fiction*
these two elements [the "reality principle" and the "pleasure
principle"] are much more intimately and intricately bound up
together than our discussion has so far managed to bring out'?
Why, now, do the authors turn to a novel such as *Emma* to find
identificatory satisfactions and evaluative judgements 'fused together to such an extent that they have become difficult to discuss
in isolation from one another'? The preceding discussion does not
consider this, even in the context of 'great literature'. Certainly
Emma is not exceptional in this respect. It is characteristic of the
work of such authors as Dickens, Tolstoy, Shakespeare or Lawrence
that we 'see events at once inside and outside the heroine's consciousness'. But it is still mistaken to describe the 'fusion' as one of

'identificatory satisfaction ["pleasure"] and evaluative judgements ["reality"]'. By putting it this way the Schools Council
authors want to suggest that the ('unpleasant') realities (such as
'the recognition of human fallibility' in *Emma*) are a kind of bitter
pill which the reader is able to swallow because of his ('pleasurable') identification with the heroine.

The Schools Council authors try to explain away, by the most
far-fetched and strained interpretations, the fact that readers of
literature willingly entertain feelings of suffering, pain, etc. They
try to do this by saying that the 'pain' is 'really' pleasure or that
the 'pain' is a way of 'disguising' pleasure and finally by saying
that if, in a novel like *Emma*, we are brought to face ('unwelcome',
'unwished for') human fallibility this is because Jane Austen blends
in enough identificatory gratification to make this palatable. The
point that they have not grasped, and which makes all this pseudo-
psychologizing unnecessary, was made in section (b) of this chapter.
The 'cognitive core' of the emotions we experience in relation to
literary works is different from that which occasions emotions in
response to real people and events. If we see or read a representation or portrayal of something sad, horrible, or fearful we willingly
entertain these possibilities precisely because we know that they
are not real. The sadness, horror, or fear we feel is that which is
appropriate to a representation. It is not surprising that we are
moved by representations of people and events, but it would be
surprising if we were moved in the same way by the fiction as we
are by the reality. There is no need to explain away why people
willingly entertain emotions such as sadness or fear other than to
say that they know that the characters and events which give rise
to these emotions are not real.

It is remarkable that the Schools Council authors are not *unaware* of the point I am making. In fact they go so far as to say
that the link or analogy between the psychoanalytic term 'identification' and the reader's experience of absorbed sympathy with a
fictional character 'unhelpfully blurs the distinction between a
feeling relationship with someone in real life and an *imagined* sympathy with a fictional character who exists only as a distillation of
the reader's contact with words on a page'.[31] This is not *quite* the
right formulation, of course. I don't *imagine* sympathy with Anna
Karenina, even though she is a product of Tolstoy's imagination,
and my only knowledge of her is through my contact with words

on a page. I feel *genuine* sympathy, but it is that which is appropriate to a representation or portrayal of a person.

Given that the Schools Council authors do show this degree of awareness of the crucial distinction between emotions in response to literature and emotions in response to life, how could they so thoroughly have lost sight of it through so much of their discussion? The key passage in which they lose track of the point is directly concerned with the issue of empathic responses to fictional characters and this is an issue which necessitates a chapter to itself. I will begin the next chapter by citing this passage.

In his essay *On Tragedy*, David Hume is surprised by the emotional reactions of the audience at a play : 'They are pleased in proportion as they are afflicted and are never so happy as when they employ tears, sobs and cries to give vent to their sorrow.'[32] I have argued that such reactions are not surprising since the audience is aware that it is being moved by representations of events. Failure to keep clear the distinction between emotional responses to literature and emotional responses to life can lead literary and educational theorists wildly astray and, as in the case of the Schools Council authors, can mislead teachers about the nature and objectives of literary education.

Plato thought that art could corrupt by nourishing the passions. Aristotle denied this and held that art gives harmless or even useful purgation; by exciting pity and fear in us, tragedy enables us to leave the theatre 'in calm of mind, all passion spent'. Whether or not W. H. Auden understood what Aristotle meant by catharsis, I think he is clearer than either Plato or Aristotle about the fundamental distinction between the emotions we experience in response to good literature or art and emotions which are occasioned by other kinds of objects :

If I understand what Aristotle means by catharsis, I can only say he is wrong. It is an effect produced, not by works of art, but by bull-fights, professional football matches, bad movies and, in those who can stand that sort of thing, monster rallies at which ten thousand girl guides form themselves into the national flag.[33]

6

Empathy and literary education

(a) Empathy and wish-fulfilment

Very central to the psychoanalytic concept of identification in real life is
the idea of an endeavour, largely unconscious, to 'mould a person's ego
after the fashion of the one that has been taken as a model. . .' Now, at
first sight, it seems inherently implausible that a moulding or modelling
of this sort (undoubtedly very important in real-life relationships) can
play a significant part in our response to the reading of fiction. Surely
it cannot reasonably be maintained that in 'identifying' with Catherine
Morland (in *Northanger Abbey*) the middle-aged male reader wants to
become like her. Yet, on reflection we can see that this difficulty arises
from a failure to differentiate clearly enough between the real world
and the fictional world. The reader who is in his right mind is fully
aware that what he is doing is reading a novel, and that in whatever
ways this activity may influence – either in the short term or the long
term – the balance of forces within his own psyche, it cannot in the real
world transform him into someone other than himself. Nevertheless,
within the fictional world constructed for him by the words of the
novelist, he may for a time be caught up by the wish to be some particular character in imagination, to share the consciousness, feelings and
experience of this character, and to gain emotional satisfaction from the
absorbed imaginative sympathy which accompanies this sharing. In this
sense the identification experienced by a reader of fiction seems to be
very intimately bound up with the kind of emotional satisfaction which
others have described as wish-fulfilment. It is true that the wishes are
gratified only in imagination, but the gratification can be intensely
pleasurable nonetheless, and it is attained by an emotional attachment
which encompasses not only empathy and recognition of similarity, but
also the wish to be temporarily like the chosen character. To return to
our specific instance, we can say that the main emotional satisfaction
which the reader derives from the relevant sections of *The Secret Agent*
is that of joining with Conrad in his authorial evaluative judgement
(compassionate, empathic, but ultimately disapproving) of Mr Verloc,
whereas the main emotional satisfaction which the reader takes from
the latter part of *Northanger Abbey* is that of joining with Catherine in
her own experiences of alarm, distress, suspense and, ultimately, relief.[1]

Let me begin by agreeing with the Schools Council authors that
one aspect of our enjoyment of *Northanger Abbey* and, indeed, of

most works of literature, is the satisfaction obtained from empathizing with or 'joining with' characters such as Catherine as they undergo the various experiences portrayed in fiction. There is a clear distinction, however, between enjoying such vicarious experiences and *the wish to be* some particular character in imagination. While we do often share, in imagination, the consciousness and feelings of characters in fiction this does not necessarily imply a wish to *be* them in imagination. One is often imaginatively 'caught up' with Humbert Humbert in *Lolita*, Raskolnikov in *Crime and Punishment*, with Macbeth, Othello and Lear, but there is *no* sense in which one wants to be them.

Furthermore, one is not caught up with *chosen* characters. The reader does not *choose* to relate more closely to Catherine (or to Emma or Dorothea or Humbert) than to other characters in the novel. This relationship is something for which the novelist is responsible. It is the author who shifts our 'point of view' and engages or disengages our sympathies with the characters she presents.

Most importantly, one is never *simply* 'caught up' with any character in the work of such novelists as Jane Austen, Conrad, Dostoevsky or Nabokov. It is a great temptation to simplify this, to reduce the complex workings of a novel such as *Northanger Abbey* to 'the emotional satisfaction of joining with Catherine'. Whereas our emotional engagement with Catherine is subtly controlled by Jane Austen so that we both see through her eyes *and* through Jane Austen's.[2] The reader never simply 'wishes to be' Catherine. Jane Austen orchestrates our response to Catherine in relation to the other characters largely through the narrative voice, which 'places' Catherine and controls the ebb and flow of the reader's sympathies. Consider the example referred to by the Schools Council authors when, according to them, we feel 'most closely identified' with Catherine.

Don't we, in fact, feel most closely identified with her at that point in the novel when she sits in the carriage which conveys her away from Northanger Abbey, feeling guilt at her own outrageous misconceptions about General Tilney, bewilderment and resentment at the disproportionate retribution meted out to her, and suspense as to the future prospects of her relationship with General Tilney's son?[3]

The Schools Council authors acknowledge that at this point our attitude to Catherine is 'a mixed one'; Catherine is aware of her own follies and so is the reader, and they conclude that 'neither admiration, nor recognition of similarity, – nor even a combination of the two – seems adequate to account for this instance of identification'. In view of this, they admit that their attempt to clarify the 'confused notion of "identification" ' in the reading process has been 'somewhat abortive'. But what they then do is to fall back on the notion of wish-fulfilment (in the long passage cited on p. 114).

'Wish-fulfilment' does not help to elucidate the emotional currents tugging at the reader at this point in *Northanger Abbey*, nor, for that matter, at any point in the novel. The kind of emotional satisfaction that is represented by simply 'joining with Catherine in her own experiences of alarm, distress, suspense and, ultimately, relief' is the kind of satisfaction that is readily obtainable from any moderately accomplished thriller or tear-jerker or romance. In fact, it is precisely this kind of fiction that Jane Austen is so acutely satirizing, most explicitly in the early pages of *Northanger Abbey*. And it is because Catherine has herself been steeped in fiction which encourages her to 'join with' stereotyped fictional heroines that she looks for 'wish-fulfilment' and indulges fantasies when she visits Northanger Abbey and makes herself look foolish to General Tilney's son. This is why she feels guilty and embarrassed as she sits in the coach taking her away from Northanger Abbey.

The first part of the novel is explicitly designed to amusedly ridicule 'wish-fulfilment' novels and to contrast *Northanger Abbey* with their indulgence in stereotyped fantasy. On the first page Jane Austen describes Catherine as a child in order to establish how unlikely it could be supposed that she was to be a 'heroine'.

She had a thin awkward figure, a sallow skin without much colour, dark lank hair, and strong features; – so much for her person; – and not less unpropitious for heroism seemed her mind. She was fond of all boy's play, and greatly preferred cricket not merely to dolls but to the more heroic engagements of infancy. . . What a strange unaccountable character! – for with all these symptoms of profligacy at ten years old, she had neither a bad heart nor a bad temper; was seldom stubborn, scarcely ever quarrelsome, and very kind to the little ones, with few interruptions of tyranny; she was moreover noisy and wild, hated confinement and cleanliness, and loved nothing so well as rolling down the green slope at the back of the house.

Throughout *Northanger Abbey* Jane Austen mocks the falsifications of the romantic 'wish-fulfilment' novel and, implicitly, the expectations of readers who are addicted to such novels (such as Catherine herself). Immediately following the point in the novel which the Schools Council authors refer to as when we most fully join with Catherine's feelings of guilt, bewilderment, resentment and suspense, and before Catherine has even left the coach, Jane Austen interpolates the following comments:

A heroine returning, at the close of her career, to her native village, in all the triumph of recovered reputation, and all the dignity of a Countess, with a long train of noble relations in their several phaetons, and their waiting maids in a travelling chaise-and-four, behind her, is an event on which the pen of the contriver may well delight to dwell; it gives credit to every conclusion, and the author must share in the glory she so liberally bestows. – But my affair is widely different; I bring back my heroine to her home in solitude and disgrace; and no sweet elation of spirits can lead me into minuteness. A heroine in a hack post-chaise, is such a blow upon sentiment, as no attempt at grandeur or pathos can withstand. Swiftly therefore shall her post-boy drive through the village, amid the gaze of Sunday groups, and speedy shall be her descent from it. (p. 188)

There is an amused astringency of tone here as Jane Austen drily denies herself the 'glory' which she might have shared with her heroine had she contrived the novel to satisfy wish-fulfilment fantasies. Jane Austen's presence in the novel as Catherine's drolly ironic 'biographer' makes it impossible to see this as being a novel in which 'the main emotional satisfaction . . . is that of joining with Catherine in her own experiences of alarm, distress, suspense and, ultimately, relief'. In fact, this novel directly *criticizes* the reader's tendency to expect such simple satisfactions. It is a criticism which is sustained throughout the novel and which thoroughly undermines the Schools Council authors' view that the emotional responses in the reader, to which the work of such authors as Jane Austen and Conrad[4] give rise, can be reduced to wish-fulfilment.

The literature teacher is working in an environment which is saturated by 'commercial' fiction and television programmes which offer readily available fantasy trips in a simple world inhabited by heroes and villains. The reader or the viewer is enabled to 'identify' with the heroes and to imaginatively 'fulfil' impossible wishes. These are simple tastes and they are easily satisfied. Children will generally prefer fiction which offers such simple satisfaction. It is often an extremely difficult task to wean children from escapist fantasy to 'serious' and 'complexly structured' works.

Literature teachers are not, fortunately, likely to be persuaded by the account which the Schools Council authors offer of *Northanger Abbey*, since it does not survive even a passing acquaintance with the novel. But it may be more difficult for teachers to resist the insidious argument that our admiration for Jane Austen's marvellous orchestration of the emotional ebb and flow we experience towards Catherine in relation to the other characters is really a superficial cover-up for the 'deeper' psychological satisfactions ('wish-fulfilment', 'the pleasure principle', etc.) that 'really' concern us, but of which we are unaware. Such arguments appear to be supported by the expertise of those, such as psychologists and psychoanalysts, who allegedly know more about what we 'really' think and feel than we are capable of knowing ourselves. In view of the widespread post-Freudian doubts about what 'really' motivates us there could easily be a receptiveness to arguments which try to reduce our perceptions of the emotional complexity of great literature to primitive satisfactions which are, allegedly, 'underneath' our 'conscious' concerns. Furthermore, such arguments go hand in glove with arguments of the kind we considered earlier, to the effect that it doesn't matter what children or adults read since it is not possible to establish that the value of one work of literature is 'objectively' superior or inferior to that of another. If all reading of fiction is 'really' or 'basically' just escapist wish-fulfilment it is pointless to indulge in literary criticism or literary education of the kind for which I have argued so far. It simply wouldn't matter what children (or adults) read, so long as they can relieve their anxieties and guilts and fulfil their fantasy wishes, and if they can accomplish these ends by other means than books, then it wouldn't matter whether or not they read at all.

It is because the Schools Council book is part of an influential series for teachers and because its reasoning can lead to such conclusions that I have given its 'theoretical considerations' such detailed scrutiny. It offers a much more fully developed argument concerning the 'emotional appeal' of literature than is commonly found in books for teachers of English and this has necessitated a quite detailed critique. The central point of the critique in this chapter has been a literary critical point (and, as such, it lays claim to the kind of objectivity which I maintained for literary critical argument in chapter 3). The example that the Schools Council authors choose to illustrate their argument, *Northanger*

Abbey, is one which supports conclusions about the 'emotional appeal' of literature which are completely contrary to the conclusions at which they arrive. The inadequacy of their argument is revealed, above all, in this complete mis-reading of the novel they refer to as a key example of 'serious' literature appealing to the reader's desire for 'wish-fulfilment'. *Northanger Abbey* is a sustained critique of escapist fantasy and wish-fulfilment, when such emotional satisfactions are all that a work of fiction offers or all that a reader is willing (or able) to receive from fiction.

It is important to say once again that I do not underestimate the difficulty that teachers face when they try to develop children's interest in, and capacity for, attentive reading of 'serious' and 'complexly structured' literature, rather than the emotional simplicities of fantasy. I have taught literature in schools where it was a considerable achievement to induce the children to read *anything*. The danger of the kind of argument I have been attacking is that it could encourage teachers to think that such achievements will suffice, that even when the educative possibilities are available to us, and we have the opportunity to interest children in great literature, there is no reason to do so, because if we analyse the value of great literature we find it reducible to wish-fulfilment gratification.

(b) Empathy with real people and empathy with characters in fiction

'Sensitivity' and 'empathy' are concepts which frequently occur in statements of the objectives of literary education. 'Sensitivity' is sometimes used to refer to a 'feel' (or a 'nose') for the subtleties and nuances of literary works. In this sense it has close connections with the concept of 'appreciation' (as in the phrase 'a sensitive appreciation') and its analysis requires a similar attention to normative, critical considerations which I have maintained are essential to an analysis of 'appreciation'.[5] If one person is said to be more sensitive than another with regard to his response to works of literature, this will be analysable largely in terms of his capacity to perceive, experience or feel in a way which is more finely tuned to 'relevant' aspects of literary works which occasion 'appropriate' perceptions, experiences and feelings. Insensitivity towards a work of literature relates to a failure to perceive/experience/feel what is 'there' in a work and this is a failing which literary education could be expected to remedy.

Special problems arise, however, when the 'sensibility' which is alleged to be developed by reading and discussing literary works is meant to relate to the development of sensitivity towards other people. It is frequently claimed that reading and discussing literary works will develop sensitivity towards other people's feelings and states of mind.

As they 'try on' first one story book character, then another, imagination and sympathy, the power to enter into another personality and situation which is characteristic of childhood and a fundamental condition of good social relationships, is preserved and nurtured. It is also through literature that children feel forward to the experiences, the hopes and fears that await them in everyday life.[6]

The concept which is most often invoked in these connections is 'empathy'. This concept has given rise to a considerable literature[7] in discussions of history, anthropology and the social sciences and it enjoyed a vogue in psychology earlier this century. A typical statement from the sphere of literary education appears in Creber's *Sense and Sensitivity* (sub-titled 'The philosophy and practice of English teaching').

in the final stage, we encourage them [the pupils] to cultivate their capacity for empathy – 'the power of projecting one's personality into, and so fully understanding, the object of contemplation'. (*Shorter O.E.D.*)
   The activity which we wish to promote is that of imaginative projection, which involves in part a projection of one's self, but also calls into play the exploration of other's experiences, other's attitudes, other states of mind. This gain in sympathy through imagination, since it can be measured only in human terms cannot be measured at all.[8]

Such claims are so common that educational philosophers are even inclined simply to take them for granted. Israel Scheffler, for example, mentions empathy almost *en passant* :

The use of literature to develop empathy is often noted. But to suppose that this function is restricted to literature is to impoverish our view of other subjects. Anthropology, history and the other human sciences also offer opportunities to empathise.[9]

I am not concerned here with the potentialities of other subjects but I think it is important to make some attempt at an analysis of the concept of 'empathy' in relation to people before I ask what might be involved in speaking of empathy in relation to works of literature.

(i) *Empathy towards other people as an 'attitude' – 'cognitive' and 'affective' dimensions in empathy*

In what follows I will argue that the analysis of the concept of 'empathy' (with other people) necessitates reference to 'cognitive' considerations and that it may not be construed merely as an 'attitude'. (Readers who are prepared to accept this are advised to skip this section and move directly to the main topic of concern – empathy with fictional personages – in the next section.)

When D. W. Hamlyn[10] distinguishes between 'knowledge that' (something is the case) and 'knowledge of persons and things' he describes the latter as being close to 'acquaintance with'. While he maintains that this implies some 'confrontation' with a person or thing, he denies that 'the direct intuition of an object' (the state of mind for which Aristotle and Plato use the term 'gnosis') goes beyond 'knowledge that'. Hamlyn argues that any such awareness could be expressed 'only in terms of what the subject knows about the object of awareness, what relevant facts he knows; hence . . . what a person knows when he has direct awareness of an object is "knowledge that" '.[11]

In this chapter on 'knowledge of oneself and others' Hamlyn maintains that 'knowledge of anything demands an understanding of the kind of thing that the object is and full knowledge requires full understanding'. Knowledge of other persons[12] presupposes knowledge of personal relationships :

A person who could not feel sympathy towards others, who could not establish relationships with them with all the dimensions of feeling that this presupposes could not ever be said to know people in the full sense. . . Some people have a kind of intuitive appreciation of these things, and are in consequence good at getting to know people.[13]

It is important to distinguish this 'kind of intuitive appreciation' of other people and of human relationships from what Jane Martin[14] refers to as 'being understanding' towards other people (which she labels 'understanding(A)'). According to Martin this is an 'attitude' which involves 'looking or at least trying to look at things through the other person's eyes and being sympathetic towards him. If someone takes this attitude consistently in a wide range of situations we refer to him as an understanding(ᴀ) person.' Martin distinguishes understanding(ᴀ) from 'understanding(c)' which she puts forward as the 'cognitive' sense of understanding. This 'cognitive' understanding is related to knowing and believing (that something is the case) and, in her view, has 'nothing to do with sympathy or identification or empathy, all of which are closely connected with *being* understanding(ᴀ)'. Martin argues at some length that being understanding is of great importance in education on the grounds that it is only by 'putting himself in other people's shoes' and 'seeing and feeling from another's position' that a student can adopt other people's ways of living, acting, seeing and feeling.

I am not concerned here with the merits or defects of this as an educational proposal. My concern is with the total separation which Martin suggests between 'being understanding' and cognitive considerations. Although Hamlyn acknowledges that there are 'affective' and even 'intuitive' elements in 'knowing other people' he is not suggesting that this form of awareness is separable from 'knowing that' or cognitive considerations. Our 'intuitive appreciations' may be right or wrong. Some people are said to be good at getting to know people because their 'intuitions' about other people's feelings and states of mind are usually right. Such people could also be said to be 'understanding sorts of people'. At least it seems a necessary condition of being an 'understanding sort of person' that one is very often right in one's judgement of other people's feelings and states of mind.

However Martin maintains that 'being understanding(ᴀ) towards other people does not require that one *succeeds* in being understanding'.[15] In her view all that is necessary for 'being understanding' is that someone *tries* to put himself in another's position (and *tries* to think and feel as he does) and that he *thinks* that he has done so. On this account it would make sense to say that someone is an 'understanding sort of person' even though he consistently misconstrues other people's thoughts and feelings (e.g. he commiserates with their pleasure and is amused by their disappointments) so long as he *tries* to empathize with them and *thinks* he has done so.

I am quite unable to see that this makes sense. If someone's attempt to empathize with others fails then he can only be granted credit for trying to empathize, not for empathizing. Empathizing and understanding (like 'winning' and 'communicating') are achievement verbs.[16] One can try to be 'an understanding sort of person', try to empathize with others, but if one fails then one is simply not an understanding sort of person.

Martin comments that 'being understanding(a) towards other people does not require rational explanation' – it is 'an attitude and not a particularly intellectual one'. This seems to indicate the source of her error. For although, as Hamlyn points out, there are 'affective' and even 'intuitive' elements in an empathic response which mean that we find it difficult to give a 'rationale' for it, we would deny that a response was an empathic response if it does not correspond in some way to the feelings and thoughts of the agent concerned.

I am claiming that an analysis of 'being understanding', 'being sympathetic', 'being empathic' necessitates attention not only to 'affective' considerations but also to a 'knowledge condition'. Since the 'knowledge condition' for each of these concepts is somewhat different[17] I will concentrate only on 'empathy' in what follows.

The point I am making may be developed further by the following example.[18] A is at a party. At one point the group he is with begin to discuss the recent road fatalities. At about this time A and his friend B see an acquaintance of theirs put his hand to his heart as a frown flickers across his face. Afterwards B tells A that he empathized with the acquaintance at that moment, for he immediately remembered that the acquaintance had lost his wife in a motor accident. If A agrees that the acquaintance had looked sad at that moment but is able to establish that neither his wife nor any family member or friend had been involved in a motor accident, would we be prepared to admit that B had empathized? Clearly not. The acquaintance may have discovered that he had left his pipe at home. It may be true that B in some sense 'knew' how the acquaintance felt (i.e. sad) but not in regard to the correct context.

Even more is required than knowing how another person feels in a given situation before we can be said to empathize with that person. It is necessary that the observer see in the situation *reason* sufficient for the person to feel as he does.

'Reason' here means nothing more elaborate than is apparent in such statements as 'he had reason to be pleased' or 'that is no reason to be angry'. We cannot empathize with someone who is angry unless we can see that the situation is such as to provide sufficient reason for anger. We might recognize that the person is angry but be puzzled by the anger because we cannot understand why the situation makes him angry. Confusion describes this situation, not empathy.[19]

With regard to the 'affective' considerations involved in empathizing it should be observed that the 'feeling' which is required for empathy is not quite the same for the observer as it is for the agent, for the observer is responding to someone responding to a situation. When John becomes angry because the traffic officer said something to his brother which angered him there comes a point, as John's anger increases, when he is no longer empathizing with his brother but is just plain angry with the traffic officer. Knowing as we do that B was scuttling round that corner in terror because the protest he was in had just been broken up by a National Guard bayonet charge, are we running down the street in terror now because we empathize with him or because we fear cold steel? It is necessary for John to see the reason for his brother's anger. It is necessary for us to know why B is terrified. But John, and we also, must be shielded from the situation to which the one we are observing is responding. To the extent that we respond directly to the stimulus instead of to the person who is reacting to the stimulus – to that extent we will not be empathizing.

My conclusion is that 'empathy' with other people must satisfy a number of 'cognitive' conditions if it is to be a genuine case of 'empathy'. The analysis has demonstrated a point made elsewhere in this book, particularly in the previous chapter, that there are logical connections between the way we feel and the way we see things. The knowledge condition and the affective condition for empathy are intimately related. It is logically impossible to feel the same sort of feeling as X does (affective condition) unless we perceive a situation in a way similar to X (knowledge condition).

If the foregoing analysis of the 'cognitive' and 'affective' dimensions involved in empathizing with other people is satisfactory we may turn to the more important question (in the context of this book) – may reading works of literature be said to promote empathy with other people?

(ii) *Empathy with characters in fiction*

I will begin by recalling Hamlyn's remark that 'knowledge of any-thing requires an understanding of the kind of thing that the object is and full knowledge requires full understanding'. In previous chapters I have argued that understanding works of literature requires an appreciation of the subtle interrelatedness of the various elements that form a literary composition. The perceptions we have of these interrelated elements (plot, character, syntax, imagery, movement, etc.) occasion emotions in the reader which are connected in multifarious ways with the emotions which are occasioned by our perceptions of real people and real events. But although we often speak of characters in fiction 'as if' they were real and often report being moved by the portrayal of their lives in ways that closely resemble the ways in which we are moved by our relations with real people, we remain aware of the funda-mental *distinctness* of actuality from representations or portrayals in literature. We do not lose sight of the fact that our emotional response to literature is occasioned by a *constructed* 'world' in which it is words on a page or actors in a theatre which produce our response. The literary orchestration of the reader's responses, to create a continually shifting 'flow and recoil of sympathy' towards what is being presented, may, in various ways, relate to or illumine our actual lives. However, the articulation of how this is achieved in particular works of literature and of the nature of the illumination makes considerable demands upon our critical capacities.

I referred earlier to some large claims which have been made for the educative value of the 'vicarious' experiences provided by literature and for the importance of empathy with fictional per-sonages. Richard Heilman[20] is also a fervent advocate of the value of literature as a means of providing us with insights into people very different from ourselves. The 'vicarious' experiences, accord-ing to Heilman, enable us to see and feel what it is like to be someone else 'from the inside'. Heilman toys a little with the idea that I have criticized – that literature is a substitute for life. 'Most modes of daily life are inevitably so constricting that any vicarious-ness may be an enlargement of the living of which the individual is capable.' But he recognizes the necessity to discriminate among the various kinds of vicarious experience which literature and film may offer. As he develops his case he refers to an example which demands much more from the reader than merely having vicarious experiences.

The more simply I can think of human truth, the easier it is to drop people into handy compartments, to make them conform to rules that suit these compartments, and above all things to deceive myself about what I am up to. In other words, the sense of human complication which is one gift from literary experience is an approach to self-knowledge, to seeing oneself in perspective, to recognizing one's doubleness of motive without falling into the opposite extreme of regarding all appearances of good as contemptible self-deceptions. Surely a student cannot work through such self-deceptions as those of Macbeth without having a door opened, if ever so narrowly, on his own share in human self-deceptiveness.[21]

The sense of human complication as it emerges in a play such as *Macbeth*, and the working through of Macbeth's self-deceptions, involve a great deal more than having vicarious experiences. While these undoubtedly play a crucial part in the flow and recoil of our sympathies towards Macbeth, as we 'enter into' and then are 'distanced' from him through Shakespeare's consummate orchestration of our responses, we are not encouraged simply to 'identify' with Macbeth or with any character in the play. Heilman's formulation of the role of empathy in literary education gains in sharpness as he acknowledges more fully the distinction between 'vicarious experience' in response to popular (or commercial) literature and the complexity of our emotional response to 'literature of quality'.

Considered in relation to knowledge, popular literature is a powerful strengthener of self-ignorance; considered in relation to feeling, popular literature simply serves to make sure that we love and hate and feel virtuous according to conventional rules that ignore the complexity of life. But literature of quality ministers to sympathy and understanding without making them too easy and without getting sloppy about it. It engages our sympathy, but keeps the object of sympathy in full perspective. It elicits at once warmth of feeling and coolness of judgement. It does not merely set us afloat on a wash of feeling, which is the way of sentimentality, or set us up high and dry on the judgement seat of principle which is the way of lecture and homily. It draws us in but it holds us out; even when we are empathically engaged, we remain contemplative onlookers.[22]

I think that Heilman over-estimates the corrupting possibilities of popular literature, and I will return to this when I consider the question of literary censorship in the final chapter. Furthermore, the fundamental distinctness of literary experience and the experiences of life for which I have argued above makes some of Heilman's claims for the morally improving effects of 'literature of quality' look extremely optimistic. But it will be apparent that Heilman's formulation of the way in which empathy works in relation to good literature bears a strong resemblance to my own attempt to formulate it in the context of *Northanger Abbey*. I think it is important to try to develop and illustrate the argument further, partly because Heilman refuses to press his case. He says,

I am not stating demonstrable propositions here, I am really talking about a faith. I would guess, in the first place that a teacher of literature at any level would need some such faith, whether its creed contain these or other articles, that literary study achieves something positive and substantial.[23]

My assumption throughout this book has been that faith is not enough and that creeds are appropriate for enterprises which are not susceptible to rational argument. Such enterprises cannot be educative ones. Heilman's refusal to insist on a serious debate about the issues he raises so well places him in the company of the proselytizers and educational fashion-mongers who tend to dominate the discussion of literary education.

I argued earlier, against the Schools Council authors, that with works of literature which we read for, and which are usually written for, 'escape' the evocation of vicarious experiences becomes an end itself. In such works we may be encouraged to lull ourselves into an 'uncritical' acceptance of 'being' a superspy, a flying ace or a great lover. It usually requires no assistance from teachers to promote such vicarious experiences – they are among the most readily available experiences that literature can offer. In fact much of the teacher's effort will be devoted to suggesting that there are other ways of responding to literature and to films than the simple and naive empathic responses to fictional personages which are encouraged by 'escapist' reading and television viewing. (It would be foolish, of course, for a teacher to try to do this too rapidly. I have acknowledged that reading works of literature is an immediately pleasurable and engrossing activity and such enjoyment is not to be despised. Considerable tact on the teacher's part is necessary if students' spontaneous interest in literature is to be extended into the more developed forms of 'critical' awareness and discrimination for which I have argued.)

With works of literature of any complexity our tendency to empathize with fictional personages is continually being checked and channelled, directed and controlled in the interests of an aesthetic 'whole'. If we consider, for example, the 'personae' of Donne's poems, of Browning's dramatic monologues, of Shakespeare's plays or of Dostoevsky's novels, to mention just a few examples, we find immensely powerful realizations of the states of mind and feeling of fictional personages which induce us to 'vicariously experience' the state of mind and feeling of, say, the lover in the 'Nocturnall on S. Lucies Day', the Duke in 'My Last Duchess', King Lear or Raskolnikov. But merely to empathize with any of these characters is to fail to grasp the subtle demands which these works make upon our feelings and sympathies. In the 'Nocturnall' for example, the powerful rhythms of desperation in the speaker's voice compel us to 'enter into' his attempts to define the 'nothingness' he experiences at the death of his love; but the images he finds or, rather, which Donne leads him to find, work subtly against our involvement until, at about the middle of the poem, we begin to see the answer to his misery, an answer which 'he' does not see until the gap between the second last and final stanza.[24] As Rosamond Tuve[25] points out, Donne's use of 'ironia' in this poem makes it one of the most intellectually demanding poems in the language. We are pulled towards and 'into' the speaker's experience at the same time as we are 'distanced' by the implication of the images. An adequate response to this poem must do justice to the tensions it sets up between a pressure towards empathy and a pressure towards detachment from the (presented) experience.

I think it is worth taking the risk of labouring this elementary critical point, that our empathic response to fictional personages is but one strand in the total structure of understanding and feeling which is occasioned by reading literary works of any complexity. In my analysis of empathy in relation to real people I emphasized the importance of 'cognitive' as well as 'affective' considerations. I argued that in order to empathize with another person it is necessary to know how another person feels in a given situation or context. With regard to works of literature, however, the 'context' or 'situation' in which the thoughts and feelings of fictional personages are presented is not, of course, that of the real world but of a composed or constructed 'world'. This 'world' is created not merely to 'reflect reality' but to order or interpret reality as part of some aesthetic purpose. Our sympathies are engaged (or disengaged) in ways that relate to the purposes of the aesthetic whole.

For example, when Antony departs from Rome (Act I, Scene iii, *Antony and Cleopatra*) a constant tension is set up between our awareness that Cleopatra is 'dissembling' (which 'distances' our response) and our awareness of her genuine grief (which promotes an 'empathic' response). We are prepared for dissimulation when Cleopatra instructs Charmian to search for Antony :

> If you find him sad,
> Say I am dancing; if in mirth, report
> That I am sudden sick.

In the course of the scene Cleopatra drives Antony almost beyond endurance. We are unprepared for her genuine grief when it breaks out (as, indeed, Shakespeare is suggesting that Cleopatra is unprepared) :

> Courteous lord, one word.
> Sir, you and I must part, but that's not it;
> Sir, you and I have loved, but there's not it :
> That you know well. Something it is I would –
> O, my oblivion is a very Antony.
> And I am all forgotten.

Even here there is an element of self-pity. John F. Danby refers to the 'deliquescent truth' of *Antony and Cleopatra* : 'The war of the contraries pervades the love too. In coming together they lapse, slide and fall apart unceasingly.'[26] The constant demands which such a work makes upon our sympathies cannot be separated from the constant demands it makes upon our 'critical' capacities. The adequacy of empathy as a response to Shakespeare's presentation of Antony or of Cleopatra is itself a matter which is subject to literary critical analysis (as it is in the case of any character in literature).

The ways in which 'literature of quality' may enlarge our sympathies and make us more aware of the possibilities of self-deception are far more various and subtle than the mere provision of 'vicarious experiences' of empathy with fictional characters.

These can be provided by Biggles and James Bond for the receptive reader. Empathizing with the goodies and rejecting the baddies simply confirms prejudice and may lead us to love and hate and feel virtuous according to conventional rules, as Heilman points out. Television serials and pulp novels encourage stereotyping and narrow their audience's sympathies by means of 'vicarious experiences' and empathy. At least they do so in so far as they *have* much actual connection with our lives and I want to conclude by returning to my doubts about whether the relationship between literature and life – between *any* literature and life – is as close as it is often claimed to be.

The ability to empathize with fictional characters is one which we exhibit on our mother's knee. This suggests that there is a crucial disjunction between our capacity to empathize with fictional characters and our capacity to empathize with real people, since small children are notoriously inept at even seeing things from someone else's point of view, let alone empathizing with them in a way that would satisfy the conditions for empathizing with real people that I advanced earlier on. The major source of this disjunction, I suggest, is that empathizing with fictional characters is not something for which *we* are responsible – it is the product of identification techniques which are readily available to any storyteller or film maker. These techniques provide the illusion of thinking the thoughts or feeling the feelings of the characters. No effort on our part is required – with the greatest of ease we slip into the character's shoes. In the case of empathizing with real people, however, considerable intellectual and moral effort is often involved. It is one thing to empathize with Humbert Humbert's adoration of eleven year old Lolita, since Nabokov (and the director of the film) make it so easy to see things from Humbert's point of view. It is quite another thing to empathize with an actual child-molester.

But wouldn't reading *Lolita* and empathizing with Humbert enlarge our sympathies and make us more capable of empathizing with child-molesters? Would empathizing with Raskolnikov make us less ready to condemn men who kill women with axes? My doubts about the likelihood of this (I leave aside the question of its desirability!) partly depend on the point I have just made, that in literature it requires no effort to empathize – the writer makes it so easy that it is difficult to see how the literary experience is a preparation for dealing with the difficult problem of empathizing with evil, or even merely antipathetic, people in real life.

The other factor which leads me to doubt the large claims that are frequently made for the value of empathizing with fictional characters as a means of developing the capacity to empathize with real people relates to a point which emerged in the previous chapter. Part of the 'cognitive core' of our empathic response to characters in novels and plays is that they are the product of artistic contrivance and this led me to suggest that there is a greater gap or disconnection between our response to literature and our response to reality than is widely supposed.

If my doubts about the morally educative value of empathizing with characters in fiction have any substance they would at least help to explain the common observation that some people who respond very sensitively to literature are highly insensitive towards other people.

7

Literary intention and literary education

References to an author's intention in the discussion of works of literature largely disappeared from literary critical currency in the 1950s, partly as a consequence of Wimsatt and Beardsley's classic paper, 'The intentional fallacy', of 1946.[1] Given the usual lag between new or altered conceptions among those at the forefront of a discipline and their adoption in schools it is only in recent years that one might expect the conceptual currency of teachers to reflect the change. A visitor to an English classroom is still likely to encounter the teacher who asks his students to decipher the intention of the author of the literary work under scrutiny, but it is less common than it used to be. Since I believe that, in general, school students ought *not* to be encouraged to seek an author's intention it concerns me that a number of philosophers and critics have tried, in recent years, to reinstate the pursuit of author's intentions as a non-fallacious and important critical enterprise. In what follows I will argue that while some of the points which have been advanced in support of intention-seeking in literature are valid, they do not warrant the re-introduction of the pursuit in the early stages of literary education. For while there are perfectly legitimate (non-fallacious) ways of referring to an author's intention in writing and critically respectable ways of determining this, these will not be readily apparent in the early stages of literary education. The young student will not have an adequate grasp of the distinctive mode of utterance that literature is and will not have a sufficiently developed notion of 'intention'. His conception of intention is likely to be restricted to what I shall call 'generative' intention and if he is encouraged to search for authors' intentions he is, as a consequence, likely to continue to misconstrue literature as a mode of discourse. The one misconception will support and reinforce the other.

(a) Generative and operative intention in literature

A member of the London Literary Club, Anthony Chamier, once asked Oliver Goldsmith 'what he meant by *slow*, the last word in the first line of *The Traveller*, "Remote, unfriended, melancholy, slow". Did he mean tardiness of locomotion? Goldsmith, who would say something without consideration, answered "yes".' But Samuel Johnson happened to be present and cut in, 'No, Sir, you do not mean tardiness of locomotion, you mean, that sluggishness of mind which comes upon a man in solitude.'[2]

Was Johnson disregarding Goldsmith's intention? Hardly, since he was asserting that Goldsmith was mistaken as to what his intention was. If, then, Goldsmith had reconsidered and ended up agreeing with Johnson would this entail that we could be sure about what Goldsmith 'really meant' by the word 'slow'? Not at all, for as an early commentator, John Forster, says, 'Who can doubt that he also meant slowness of motion? The first point of the picture is *that*. The poet is moving slowly, his tardiness of gait measuring the heaviness of heart, the pensive spirit, the melancholy of which it is the outward expression and sign.'[3] Wimsatt, who cites this example, observes that although Goldsmith is closer to the 'generative intention' of his own poem than others, he is not therefore a better critic or commentator. If Forster seems better than Johnson in this instance, 'the grounds of his judgement and ours must lie in the observable force and relevance of the word "slow" in the *context* of the first line of Goldsmith's pensive travelogue'.

'Generative intention' or what the author 'had in mind' when he composed is to be distinguished from 'effective' or 'operative' intention as it appears in the completed work. Johnson's challenge to Goldsmith sounds arrogant because of the implicit play on these two senses of 'intention' (or 'what the writer meant'). If Goldsmith *did* have tardiness of locomotion in mind then that was his generative intention and he is in a privileged position to assert this. But of course there are all kinds of nuances, complexities and subtleties in literature to which the author may not have attended as he wrote. This does not mean that they are unintentional, in the sense that they are accidental. Often the most productive areas of our thought are at the periphery of what we are focusing on. Good ideas sometimes 'come' unexpectedly and tangentially to our most conscious and deliberated concerns. This does not make them accidental or any less 'ours', any more than the extraordinary complexity and subtlety of Shakespeare's verse is accidental, although he could not have been 'attending to' or 'conscious of' all that is to be found in his work.

D. W. Harding suggests that if our interpretation of a work of literature goes altogether beyond what the author could possibly have been aware of we lose the social relation between ourselves and him. He maintains that if what we enjoy in a work of art is unconnected with the artist's satisfaction, 'the work becomes an unintended feature of the world, non social, like a sunset or a canyon, beautiful perhaps but not mediating contact with a human maker'.[4] It seems as if Harding is here referring to the artist's *actual* satisfaction and the obvious objection to this is that the artist may be unaware of aspects of his own work which, had they been pointed out to him, could have given him new sources of satisfaction. Harding tightens his formulation later on.

But when the work is known to be by one particular author it seems impossible to disregard the limitations of what he could have seen in it himself. Where we can see more modern applications of what he wrote we can no doubt fully accept them as part of the meaning his work would have implied if he had been writing later; we simply grasp in terms of our own institutions and familiar events what the author had understood in terms of institutions and events that had a parallel significance for him. Much of Voltaire's *Candide*, for instance, has this sort of contemporary relevance, and no doubt some of *Don Quixote* as Madariaga claims. The question is where to draw the line, and the reader's practised judgement must be his guide in every instance. If we accept too much of the time-added meanings we are going in the direction of the medieval writers who claimed that a passage of Virgil was an unconscious prophecy of the birth of Christ; we depart too far from any meaning that the work could possibly have had for its author, and we lose the possibility of sharing in his satisfaction with the finished work.

So long as the author's 'satisfaction' is entertained by Harding as possibly stemming from 'any meaning that the work could possibly have had for its author' we avoid the far too restrictive limitation of the author's *actual* satisfaction with his work. I do not think that we can restrict our interpretations further than 'the limitations of what he *could have* seen in it himself'.

Sometimes an artist is reluctant to accept readings of his work which to others are manifestly acceptable. We might assume, for example, that Milton would be most reluctant to accept a reading of *Paradise Lost* which sees Satan as the hero. Yet that is the way it has been interpreted by a succession of highly 'practised' readers since Dryden. In a non-literary context, Robin Wood concludes a penetrating analysis of Alfred Hitchcock's film *Psycho* with these remarks.

No film conveys . . . a greater sense of desolation, yet it does so from an exceptionally mature and secure emotional standpoint. And an essential part of this viewpoint is the detached sardonic humour. It enables the film to contemplate the ultimate horrors without hysteria, with a poised, almost serene detachment. This is probably not what Hitchcock meant when he said that one cannot appreciate *Psycho* without a sense of humour, but that is what he *should* have meant. He himself – if his interviews are to be trusted[5] – has not really faced up to what he was doing when he made the film. This, needless to say, must not affect one's estimate of the film itself. For the maker of *Psycho* to regard it as a 'fun' picture can be taken as his means of preserving his sanity; for the critic to do so – and to give it his approval on these grounds – is quite unpardonable. Hitchcock (again if his interviews are to be trusted) is a much greater artist than he knows.[6]

There seems to be a large step involved in moving from Harding's limitation on the range of our interpretations (what the artist 'could have' seen in it himself) to Wood's, what the artist 'should have' seen in it himself. Wood's comment seems to be arrogant in the way Johnson's comment on Goldsmith seemed to be arrogant. However, Wood is suggesting, in effect, that Hitchcock has to cling to his 'generative' intention (to make a fun picture) for very powerful personal reasons (to preserve his sanity).[7] Wood is certainly not suggesting that the profound and serious aspects of *Psycho* become, as a consequence, 'unintended features of the world, like sunsets or canyons'. Hitchcock 'had not really faced up to what he was doing when he made the film', i.e. he *was* responsible for the effective or operative intentions which become apparent to Wood as he views the film. Wood also insists on the possibility that Hitchcock's own testimony is not to be trusted.[8]

'Never trust the artist – trust the tale' overstates, in D. H. Lawrence's inimitable fashion, an important truth. We usually have no choice but to trust the artist regarding his generative intention, although Hitchcock provides an interesting counterexample, since he may be deceiving us about this (either deliberately, to poke fun at the critics, or from a kind of psychological necessity). But there is no reason why we should trust the artist concerning the 'operative' or 'effective' intention manifested in the completed work.

Most critics are reluctant to break altogether the connection between generative and operative intention. Thus Robin Wood leaves open the possibility that Hitchcock could be brought to see his operative intention. If he could not, this is something that requires explanation (e.g. the implications of the film are too disturbing for him to contemplate). Or maybe he *is* aware of his operative intention but is deceiving us.

A similar effort to retain a link between generative and operative intention was made by Edmund Wilson in his account of Henry James' story *The Turn of the Screw* : Wilson argued that the ghosts in the story were figments of the governess's imagination and that James had not intended to imply their 'objective' existence in the story. When James' notebooks were published it became clear that James had consciously intended to produce a ghost story. Wilson nevertheless insisted that it is a study in the neurotic effects of repressed sexuality. He argued, on the basis of certain biographical facts about James, that 'in *The Turn of the Screw* not merely is the governess self-deceived but that James is self-deceived about her. The doubt that some readers feel as to the soundness of the governess's story are the reflections of doubts communicated unconsciously by James himself.'

Frank Cioffi offers this as an example of 'an implicit biographical reference in our response to literature. It is only when it is missing that we notice that it was always there'.[9] The suggestion is that Wilson has to insist that James was self-deceived about his operative intention if the features of the story detected by Wilson are not to become 'unintended features of the world like a sunset or a canyon'. 'The suspicion that a poetic effect is an accident is fatal to the enjoyment which literature characteristically offers.'[10]

We can accept that if an effect is demonstrably gratuitous or accidental then it is critically inadmissible. But it is not often very easy to establish this. Certainly Virgil could not have intended, in any sense of the term, to have prophesied the birth of Christ, nor could my five year old daughter have intended to incorporate in her story references to an Icelandic text which has not been translated into English, despite the striking resemblances. The 'appearance' of such 'references' in Virgil or the child's story is accidental and cannot be allowed to enter into our interpretation of what they have written. There can be no question in either case that the authors 'could have' or 'should have' seen such references in what they have written.

In general, we are not in a position to assert that a writer *could not* have (operatively) intended the presence of features of his work which are apparent to the reader. In odd cases the author may be more reluctant than most to acknowledge them, however, and may cling tenaciously to his generative intention and resist the interpretation. There needs to be no 'biographical reference' to support the interpretation if it is a good one. Wilson only *needs* biographical evidence to support his account of *The Turn of the Screw* if there is room for (critical) doubt about the adequacy of his interpretation. *Psycho* is not just a 'fun picture' no matter what Hitchcock says or what his biography shows. There is room for doubt about some features of the film[11] but not about whether the film's operative intention is profound and serious, as Wood makes clear. Biographical information or the author's testimony will usually be enough to establish generative intention but such information will only undermine a well supported critical account of the operative intention (which is 'realized' in the work), if it can be shown that it was empirically impossible that the author could have entertained the intention. If such evidence is not available the author is on the same footing as the critic with regard to the operative intention of his work – he will have to demonstrate in what way the critical account is unsatisfactory in relation to the account he wants to offer himself.

Some writers on literary intention become impatient with this sort of argument. George Watson, for example, reasserts Wordsworth's claim that a poet is a man speaking to men. 'In rare and memorable instances people do say remarkable things without meaning them. But anyone who conducted his social life on the principle that conversation is worth listening to only or merely for the sake of such instances would be guilty of continuous discourtesy.'[12] However Watson's conception of the issue is too coarse and serves only to bluster. The critic who advances a well argued analysis of a poem which does justice to its intricacy but which conflicts with or goes way beyond the author's stated intention is not claiming that the author is saying remarkable things without meaning them. He is saying that the author has not attended closely enough to what he meant or intended. There is a crucial difference between an 'unintended' and an 'unattended' meaning. Even in ordinary conversation there are continually present aspects of our 'meaning' to which we do not attend but which are nevertheless attended to by others. We are often poor critics of our own meaning. We frequently claim that people 'take us up the wrong way' when what has happened is that we have not attended to the non-verbal aspects of what we have said. In chapter 1 I discussed the way in which tone, volume and inflection of voice, gesture, hesitation, facial expression, etc. are orchestrated with the words we employ and interact 'organically' with them to produce a distinctive 'whole'. These aspects of our speech acts can transform 'conciliation' into 'covert aggression' or 'admiration' into barely concealed envy. When we protest that we didn't mean (intend) to be aggressive or envious we are referring to our generative intention. All too often, when we have it pointed out to us, we have to admit that the operative or effective intention could more justly be described as aggression or envy.

Just as we may discover our operative intentions when what we say is subjected to the scrutiny of others, so may the author be led to such a discovery. In fact this is even more likely to be so in the case of writers, such as W. H. Auden, who see writing as a process of discovering meaning. ('How do I know what I think till I see what I say?' as Auden put it.) The Australian novelist Xavier Herbert expressed gratitude to Vincent Buckley, a critic who had reviewed his novel *Capricornia*, by saying that he had shown him what his novel was about. Cases of this kind can be multiplied and they help to identify more clearly what is implied by referring to an author's 'operative' intention. They also raise doubts about the usefulness and advisability of any widespread re-introduction of talk of authorial intention in literary criticism and literary education.

On the account I have offered, to say that 'a work of literature manifests or realizes its author's "operative" intention' is to say no more than 'a work of literature manifests/realizes whatever it manifests/realizes', with the sole proviso that it must be empirically possible for the author to have entertained the interpretation. This account enables us to say that works of literature are not un-intentional even when we entertain interpretations of them which were not entertained by their authors. But to put it positively and

to maintain that works of literature express their authors' (operative) intentions is fraught with risk because it *suggests* more than it seems. It suggests that to look for an author's intentions is to do something different from an analysis of what the work manifests/realizes and it puts the author right back in the centre of the critic's attention. The danger of this, it seems to me, is that works of literature may consequently be viewed as expressing the *author's* thoughts and feelings (even though, of course, these may be unacknowledged by him).

And what on earth is wrong with that, I may be asked. Surely works of literature *do* express the author's thoughts and feelings. My reply is, 'not in the ordinary sense'. The sense in which it *is* so is only available to the reader who attends to the myriad ways in which authors may entertain or play with the words, characters, thoughts, rhythms, line-stops, punctuation marks, etc. that he has in his employ. I am referring, of course, to points I have argued earlier. The writer is an artist as well as 'a man speaking to men' and the thoughts/feelings/intentions which are found in his work relate to the author as artist and as man in highly complex ways. To recall yet again the (far from ordinary) sense in which T. S. Eliot relates the 'experience' in a literary work to the author :

We may have to communicate – if it is communication, for the word may beg the question – an experience which is not an experience in the ordinary sense, *for it may only exist,* formed out of many personal experiences ordered in some way which may be very different from the way of valuation of practical life, *in the expression of it.* If poetry is a form of 'communication', yet that which is to be communicated is the poem itself and only incidentally the experience and thought which have gone into it. The poem's existence is somewhere between the writer and the reader; it has a reality which is not simply the reality of what the writer is trying to 'express' or of his experience in writing it or of the experience of the reader or of the writer as reader. Consequently the problem of what a poem 'means' is a good deal more difficult than at first appears.[13]

It is clearly insufficient in the course of interpreting a work of literature to look for correspondences between an author's 'experiences', 'thought' or 'intentions' which pre-date the work and the completed work (though these may be valuable aids to interpretation). It is to assume too close a correspondence between the author as a man and the author as an artist and to ignore the possibility that the artist's concern with 'life' may be largely 'aesthetic'.

Certain moral and emotional concerns may generate a work of literature but as they become ordered and shaped in a novel or poem, 'getting it right' may lead to changes of direction or to transformation of the original concerns. The original concerns become, as it were, raw materials, along with anything else in the author's actual or imagined experience that is useful to the composition.

This development of the argument against the sufficiency of generative intention as a basis for interpretation also suggests the way in which it may be misleading to maintain that a work of literature operatively manifests the *author's* thoughts, feelings or intentions. Most literature *dramatizes* thoughts, feelings and intentions which are not the author's or not wholly the author's – it entertains and plays out possible experiences which are not necessarily, or not simply, those of the author. This can easily be lost sight of by those who maintain that works of literature are an expression of their authors' operative intention, as I will now attempt to demonstrate.

(b) Against intention

The recent revival of interest in authors' (operative) intentions reflects, in part, the influence of philosophers such as Grice, Anscombe and Austin. The point is made that an author's intention is manifested *in* what he writes – a point which was never denied by those who had referred to 'the intentional fallacy' but one which they had not, perhaps, sufficiently emphasized. I say 'perhaps' because I think there are a number of reasons why critics and teachers of literature ought, in fact, to be very circumspect about employing the notion of 'intention' in the course of their criticism or their teaching, even when they have 'operative' intention in mind. I will first of all draw attention to some difficulties which can arise in criticism when 'intention' becomes a focus. I will then be able more clearly to identify the difficulties which occur in the teaching of literature.

Accounts of an author's 'operative' intention are based on what the critic finds to be 'realized' in works of literature; but there are good reasons why the critic would be well advised to focus on what is realized and to steer clear of intention. Frank Cioffi,[14] for example, has disdainfully dismissed 'the intentional fallacy' but his attempt to revive 'intention' as a critical tool leads him into fallacious judgements. I argued earlier that reference to an author's generative intention will only undermine a convincing critical account of what is realized in a work of art if it can be shown that it was empirically impossible that the author could have entertained the account that the critic offers. It is this point which Cioffi misconceives and since it is the central contention of the first part of this chapter it should help to elaborate it if I discuss Cioffi's examples in some detail.

Example 1. Eliot and Marvell. In their original paper Wimsatt and Beardsley maintain that when Prufrock (in T. S. Eliot's 'The Love Song of J. Alfred Prufrock') asks, 'would it have been worth while. . . To have squeezed the universe into a ball', 'his words take half their sadness and irony from certain energetic and passionate lines of Marvell's "To His Coy Mistress" '. Cioffi comments that if they had incorporated the allusion to Marvell's lines[15] without knowing whether Eliot was alluding to it,

> it is doubtful whether their appreciation would have survived the discovery that he was not. If a critical remark is one which has the power to modify our apprehension of a work, then biographical remarks can be critical. They can serve the eliminative function of showing that certain interpretations of a work are based on mistaken beliefs about the author's state of knowledge.[16]

One must assume that the 'biographical remarks' would be something like Eliot saying, 'I've never read Marvell's poem' or, 'Yes, I see what you mean about the apparent connection between what I wrote and what Marvell wrote but I did not intend such a connection to be entertained by the reader.' If he were to say the former I think we would have to disbelieve him. He refers to the poem elsewhere in his criticism and unless he could furnish us with an extraordinary story to explain why he would want to deceive those who read his criticism (and why a man whose knowledge of literature is vast should have avoided one of the major poems in English) we would take the denial to be some kind of esoteric joke or whim. Even if he were to *convince* us that he had not actually read the poem we would still hypothesize that he had heard the lines quoted somewhere and not realized their source. This would be preferable to supposing that the ironic and sad appositeness of the allusion to Marvell's lines in the context of 'Prufrock' is accidental. The biographical testimony would not serve the eliminative function Cioffi suggests.

Example 2. Donne and the new astronomy. Cioffi takes another example from Wimsatt and Beardsley's paper in order to illustrate what he means by 'the eliminative function of biographical data'. John Donne's 'A Valediction : Forbidding Mourning' contains these lines :

> Moving of th' earth brings harmes and feares,
> Men reckon what it did and meant,
> But trepidation of the spheares,
> Though greater farre, is innocent.

Wimsatt and Beardsley criticize an interpretation of this quatrain which, basing itself on the biographical fact that Donne was intensely interested in the new astronomy and its theological repercussions, sees in the phrase 'Moving of th' earth' an allusion to the recently discovered motion of the earth round the sun. Wimsatt and Beardsley show the unlikelihood of this through an analysis of the text. Cioffi concedes that they make it very plausible that Donne was alluding not to the heliocentric theory of the earth's motion but to earthquakes. But, Cioffi asks, 'have they established that Donne was not referring to the motion of the earth round the sun as persuasively as our belief in Donne's ignorance of the heliocentric theory would establish it? Wouldn't this "external" fact outweigh all their "internal" ones?' The rather tortured phraseology of this question reflects Cioffi's reluctance to ask a more obvious one : 'If we established that Donne had never heard of earthquakes would we not reject Wimsatt and Beardsley's interpretation?' The answer to this is clearly affirmative but the assumption is, of course, wildly improbable. It is *less* implausible to consider the possibility that Donne was ignorant of the heliocentric theory but we would need powerful evidence to this effect if this was incompatible with the evidence in his poetry. We would need, in fact, a demonstration that it was empirically impossible for Donne to have been acquainted with the theory and it is difficult to envisage how such a demonstration could be offered in this case. We can be certain that Donne did not intend to incorporate any reference to black holes in 'trepidation of the spheares', whatever 'internal' evidence is offered by the critic. But reference to what the author could, as a matter of empirical possibility, have

intended will not *eliminate* the vast majority of critical inter-pretations.

It is important to distinguish between evidence of what the author *could*, as a matter of empirical possibility, have entertained and ('biographical') evidence of what he did (or did not) actually entertain. The former is much more coercive on our interpretation than the latter because the former embraces both generative *and* operative intention. If we establish as a biographical fact that Donne *did* not entertain an interpretation of his poem which sees in it references to the heliocentric theory we have only established something about his generative intention (what he 'had in mind' when he wrote the poem). It still remains open to the critic to argue that Donne was unaware of this aspect of his operative intention (which is 'realized' in the poem). If, on the other hand, we establish that it is unlikely that Donne *could* (empirically pos-sibly) have entertained the interpretation we also establish that any critical interpretation of what is realized in the work which makes reference to the heliocentric theory is unlikely. This does not, of course, *eliminate* the interpretation but if the evidence is strong it is much more powerful as evidence against an otherwise convincing critical interpretation than merely establishing that Donne did not, in fact, embrace the interpretation. Even if we were to establish that Donne explicitly *rejected* the interpretation this is not, in itself, sufficient to eliminate the interpretation if the interpretation is (critically) convincing. When we rejected Hitch-cock's account of *Psycho* we were denying that an author or a director is in a privileged position with regard to judgements about the operative intention of his work.

We have distinguished two ways in which we might try to eliminate or undermine an interpretation. Cioffi confuses them by referring to them both as the use of 'biographical data'. It is not a matter of 'biographical data' that eliminates the interpretation of Blake's 'Jerusalem' as expressing Fabian sentiments in the refer-ence to 'dark Satanic mills'. The fact that there were no industrial mills when Blake wrote the poem certainly eliminates the inter-pretation. But it eliminates it because it was *empirically impossible* for Blake to have referred to something of which he could have no knowledge. This cannot be construed as 'biographical data' about Blake.

Furthermore, it is not a biographical matter that a compositor's error led to the misprint of 'Soldier Aristotle' for 'Solider Aristotle' in the sixth stanza of Yeats' 'Among Schoolchildren'. As Cioffi himself admits, 'it might be objected that this is not to the point [i.e. does not help to demonstrate the eliminative function of biographical data] because the case is one of a discrepancy between what the author wrote and what we made of it and not between what he meant and what we made of it'. 'Soldier Aristotle' is unacceptable not because Yeats *did* not entertain this interpretation but because he *could* not have entertained this interpretation. It is not empirically possible for Yeats to have meant 'Soldier' when he wrote 'Solider'.[17]

Cioffi has two remaining examples which are designed to illustrate 'the eliminative function of biographical data'. In neither case is this function demonstrated since each example relies on an author's statement of his generative intention. Such statements cannot by themselves eliminate interpretations of operative intention – the author cannot be accepted as the final authority on his work. I have argued that the author is on the same footing as the critic with regard to the operative intention of his work. He can quickly eliminate mistaken versions of his generative intention since he *is* the authority on this, but he has to argue critically if he wishes to dispute an account of the operative intention of his work. It is insufficient for Housman to simply 'reveal' that his poem '1887' is not an anti-imperialist jibe. He has to persuade us that there is less justification for the reader interpreting it in this way than there is for the interpretation he originally (or generatively) intended. In this case it is relatively easy for the author to persuade us. Frank Harris, who interpreted the poem as an anti-imperialist jibe, said, 'How was I to know that someone steeped in a savage disgust of life could take pleasure in outcheapening Kipling at his cheapest?' This overstatement cannot be considered to be a strong or convincing critical argument about the poem. It is easy for Housman to demonstrate that the poem expresses patriotic sentiments (and that such sentiments are not alien to him). This is not a case where 'biographical revelation' eliminates a convincing critical interpretation but rather a weakly supported interpretation being overridden by a superior one. The fact that Housman does not argue for his interpretation disguises the source of the persuasive power of his judgement which is not that of authorial authority but that of critical plausibility. No doubt

Housman, like Cioffi, thinks it is sufficient for him to 'reveal' the intention of his poem. But we only *accept* this revelation because it is more critically plausible than Harris' interpretation. (Compare the difficulty that Milton would have in persuading us that Satan is not given heroic stature in *Paradise Lost*. No 'biographical revelations' would be sufficient to eliminate the critical interpretations which convincingly affirm that Satan does, operatively, have heroic stature in the poem.)

The remaining example which Cioffi employs to illustrate 'the eliminative function of biographical data' concerns Hopkins' note on his poem 'Henry Purcell'. Of a possible interpretation of the poem Hopkins says, 'My lines will yield a sense that way indeed, but I never meant it so.' This is a definitive statement of Hopkins' generative intention. It would take a more detailed case, however, to establish that the interpretation was an *illegitimate* interpretation of the operative intention as it is realized in the poem, especially if it was part of a convincing critical interpretation of the poem.[18]

Cioffi's ostensible point in his paper is a 'logical' one, to the effect that an implicit biographical reference is, as it were, part of our concept of literature. 'The notion of an author's intention is logically tied to the interpretation we give to his work.' So that in those cases where we persist in an interpretation which an author has rejected what we are really doing is favouring one criterion of intention as against another. When we override an author's avowed intention what we are doing is not to say that the effect we value is accidental but to say that the author was mistaken about what his intention was. Stated thus, the argument is unobjectionable. In Cioffi's critical practice, however, this revival of a concern for the author's intention too easily leads to an inflation of the importance of generative intention at the expense of a concern for what is (operatively) realized in the work.

My case against an intentionalist revival in criticism is largely based on the contention that it will create more confusion and difficulty than it will resolve, and that such confusion is apparent even in the work of the revivalist leaders. However my case is not assisted by some confusion among my anti-intentionalist allies. Since what I am arguing may more clearly emerge by contrasting it with what I am *not* arguing, the following passage is worth consideration.

> But his [the author's] intentions are no use to us: if he did what he intended to do, his intentions will be realized in his work and we do not need to ask him; if he failed to do what he intended to do, his intentions are irrelevant to our interest in his actual performance.[19]

Richard Harland has recently pointed out that we may use the evidence of what the writer does say as evidence for what was not actually said. In the case of Coleridge's poem 'Christabel', he argues, we should have no difficulty in recognizing from the text alone that the original intention was not fulfilled. In fact if we do not so regard it the poem would be 'incomprehensibly pointless'. 'We can only understand and explain what was written on the hypothesis that what was actually written was not the whole of what was originally intended.' Harland argues strongly, in the post-Wittgensteinian tradition, against the 'mental picture' model of intention :

> we need not refer this unfulfilled area of the original intention to a picture of the unwritten remainder of the poem that Coleridge realized privately but did not communicate. It is at least more likely that Coleridge did not finish *Christabel* because he was unable to form any such satisfactory picture of the remainder of the poem. Our claim that something further *should* have taken place in the public product involves no claim that a something further *did* take place secretly within the writer's own mind. For the critic, an unfulfilled intention is a visible absence, not an invisible presence.[20]

In this way even unfulfilled intentions may be determined ultimately by reference to the text rather than to biographical sources. If Coleridge had claimed in his journal that the poem was complete we would distrust the claim. We would prefer to believe that Coleridge was, for example, referring to a completed draft that had been lost rather than accept that he thought an 'incomprehensibly pointless' work was complete.

Much confusion can be avoided if critics steer clear of 'intention' and refer instead to what is (or is not) 'realized' in works of literature. As it happens I think this *is* common critical practice. It is mainly the philosophers who have stirred up the mud. It would be unfortunate if an intentionalist revival initiated by such philosophers started seeping into classrooms just when a healthy attention to what is 'realized' in literary works has become more or less dominant. It is of no avail for these philosophers to protest that in their sense an author's intention is manifested *in* what he writes.

This was a point that Wimsatt and Beardsley were right not to emphasize. When the author's intention is reasserted as a focus of critical concern, even those who profess to be able to do so without confusion succumb to error. My discussion of Cioffi's examples demonstrates that even those who profess disdain for Wimsatt and Beardsley's account of 'the intentional fallacy' can sink into conceptual quagmires of the kind that Wimsatt and Beardsley were warning against. There is good reason to suggest that many literary critics, English teachers and schoolchildren who follow Cioffi's lead will sink even deeper into the intentionalist morass.

In the context of literary education there are formidable risks to run. 'Operative' intention is a notion which is likely to be particularly confusing to those who are at an early stage of their literary education. They are very likely to be over-impressed by evidence of an author's intention drawn from outside the work – by an author's own statements, by biographical data and so on – even if their teachers advise them that in most circumstances the work itself is the best indication of an author's intention. Young students of literature are naturally inclined to treat works of literature as a form of direct communication between the author and the reader, to see him as 'a man speaking to men'. They are unlikely to be sensitive to the ways in which authors such as Donne, Marvell and Pope employ dramatic speakers in their work. They are likely to seize on key characters in works by writers such as D. H. Lawrence and to see them expressing Lawrence's 'own' views rather than to attend to the way in which what Lawrence 'intends' in his novels necessitates a response to the complex interactions between characters such as Birkin, Ursula, Gudrun and Gerald. Responding alertly to what Lawrence called 'the flow and recoil of sympathy' between the characters (and between the characters and the reader) is the *only* way of grasping Lawrence's (operative) intention in *Women in Love, Sons and Lovers* and *The Rainbow*. To invite young students to seek the 'intention' of such an author is likely to be understood as an invitation to look for a 'message', an 'aim', an idea which precedes the work and which the work is designed to 'illustrate'. With works of any complexity such an approach is fatal to an adequate apprehension or appreciation.

Even though intention-seeking has largely been in critical disrepute since Wimsatt and Beardsley's paper it is still not uncommon to hear even recently graduated teachers treat literary works as puzzles to be solved, the key to the puzzle lying in 'what the author intended' or 'what the author was trying to say'. Students are still asked questions such as, 'What was the author trying to say?' followed by 'How does he manage to say it?' The impression given by such questions is that the authors whose works are under scrutiny (Shakespeare, Dickens, Jane Austen) are peculiarly incapable of clear communication and find it necessary to dress up or obscure their 'meaning' with an ingenious and baffling array of verbal contrivances which the unfortunate student must strip away if he is to answer the teacher's question. This is, of course, literary mis-education in full bloom. In the past it has been nurtured and sustained by giving undue prominence to misconceived notions of authorial intention. While some of the misconceptions might have been eliminated in recent years, authorial intention remains an elusive and potentially misleading notion. There is little to gain and, potentially at least, a lot to lose by giving it prominence in literary education.

8

Literature, morality and censorship

AESCHYLUS:	(*To Euripides*) What are the qualities that you look for in a good poet?
EURIPIDES:	Technical skill – and he should teach a lesson, make people into better citizens.
AESCHYLUS:	And if you have failed to do this? If you have presented good men, noble men, as despicable wretches, what punishment do you think you deserve?
DIONYSIUS:	Death. No good asking him.
AESCHYLUS:	Well, now, look at the characters I left him. Fine, stalwart characters, larger than life, men who didn't shirk their responsibilities. . . I depicted men of valour, lion-hearted characters like Patrocles and Teucer, encouraging the audience to identify themselves with these heroes when the call to battle came. *I* didn't clutter *my* stage with harlots like Phaedra or Stheneboea. No one can say I have ever put an erotic female into any play of mine.
EURIPIDES:	How could you? You've never met one.
AESCHYLUS:	And thank heaven for that. Whereas you and your household had only too much experience of Aphrodite, if I remember rightly.
DIONYSIUS:	He's got you there Euripides. See what happened in your own home when you made other men's wives behave like that on stage.
EURIPIDES:	And did I invent the story of Phaedra?
AESCHYLUS:	No, no, such things do happen. But the poet should keep quiet about them, not put them on the stage for everyone to copy. Schoolboys have a master to teach them, grownups have the

poets. We have a duty to see that what we teach
them is right and proper.

(Aristophanes. *The Frogs*, 405 B.C.[1])

(In 1955 in the U.S.A. the *Lysistrata* of Aristophanes was judged to be
'plainly obscene' and 'well calculated to deprave the morals of persons reading
same and almost equally certain to arouse libidinous thoughts'.[2])

It is often noted in discussions of censorship that those who want
censorship are always concerned to protect others – those who are
impressionable, weak, easily tempted or led astray. This moral
protectionism or moral paternalism involves an assumption that
literature and art have profound effects on the emotions and beliefs
of readers and viewers, particularly wives and children. The
Crown Prosecutor, in his opening address at the British trial concerning *Lady Chatterley's Lover*[3] in 1960 asked the jurors, 'Is it a
book which you would even wish your wives or your servants to
read?' After the English edition of *Ulysses*[4] had been circulating
freely in Australia for four years, the Australian Minister for
Customs decided to examine the book and admitted to a powerful,
if unusual, personal impact. What he read made 'his hair stand on
end' and he re-imposed the ban. Mr Harrison said that the book
'holds up to ridicule the Creator and the Church. It ridicules the
whole moral standard of civilization, citizenship and decency.'
More immediately, however, 'such books might vitally affect the
standard of Australian home life'.[5]

When the majority report of the American Commission on
Obscenity and Pornography (1969–70) questioned the ability of
pornography to corrupt there was an immediate response from the
President of the U.S.A. :

I have evaluated the Report and categorically reject its morally bank-
rupt conclusions and majority recommendations. The Commission
contends that the proliferation of filthy books and plays has no lasting
effects on a man's character. If that be true, it must also be true that
great books, great paintings and great plays have no ennobling effect on
a man's conduct. Centuries of civilization and ten minutes of common-
sense will tell us otherwise.[6]

It is, perhaps, unfortunate that the spokesman for the ennobling
effect of good literature should be President Nixon. Nevertheless
this form of argument appears again in a report of a sub-committee
of the Longford Committee Investigating Pornography in Britain :

If what men read and view has no effect whatever on them, then why do industry and commerce spend millions of pounds each in advertising. . . ? Again, why do the Government and individual parents spend millions of pounds on education and why do teachers try to inculcate in their pupils a critical taste and a love of good literature, beautiful pictures and fine plays?[7]

I must admit to some degree of nervousness in arguing as I have, that bad literature is less likely to deprave and good literature less likely to ennoble than is assumed by many educators. For the next question may well be, are these millions of pounds devoted to literary education well spent? How could we convince those who draw an analogy between the money spent on advertising and the money spent on literary education that the value of a literary education is not to be measured in terms of a narrowly conceived 'moral improvement' but in far more complex ways?

The task is made even more difficult when it becomes apparent that *opponents* of the censor's 'moral protectionism' sometimes seem to share the censor's belief that books may have powerful effects on the emotions and beliefs of their readers. Geoffrey Dutton, who is most hostile to 'moral protectionism', suggests that it is hardly surprising that the censors are 'obsessed by sex . . . it is no wonder, with all the filthy books, plays, films and paintings they are exposed to'.[8] Unfortunately this jibe is at odds with the main point that Dutton wants to establish, that literature cannot lead people astray. Difficulties and confusions concerning the relationship between literature and life are most commonly aired in debates over censorship as is apparent in these passages from Dutton's contribution to the debate :

Art is basically subversive, as all political and moral censors know. Artists do not set out to convert or corrupt, but to create. Being free spirits they cannot imagine that it will hurt anyone else to be free too. Byron, who was accused at various times of corrupting England's religion with *Cain*, her politics with *The Vision of Judgement* and her sexual morals with *Don Juan* (a fine record, to score all three), wrote to his publisher John Murray in amazement: 'Do you really think such things ever led anybody astray? *Who* was ever altered by a poem?' Byron (of all people) was hardly likely to underestimate the power of the written word. All good writing, of course, is eminently censorable, as Plato pointed out long ago, in that it creates a world where good and bad exist, and the censor (like Plato) will want to keep people of impressionable mind, which is usually everyone except the censor, away from the bad and feed them only the good. But Byron was right.

Literature can certainly arouse desires, stimulate awareness, enrage, soothe, exalt, depress, but there was no evidence in his day nor is there now that it can lead anyone astray or, as he puts it, alter anyone.

A reading of *Fanny Hill* will not make a good woman into a whore, any more than a reading of the Old Testament will make a sinner obey the Ten Commandments.

Literature is not life. . .

A charming and even simpler answer comes from a lady called Fanny, in a dialogue with her friend Katy, in *The School of Venus*, or 'the Ladies' Delight Reduced into Rules of Practice', London, 1744. When Katy is 'telling in every particular' her encounter with a young man, Fanny suddenly cries out, 'This relation makes me mad for fucking!'

In some variation or other of Fanny's simple proposition, this is exactly what every good book or film or play should do. It should make its audience mad for laughter, or grief, or joy. And in societies where there is political or religious censorship, mad for freedom and justice. In Australia the censors are afraid of only one thing. But it really does not seem very likely that the whole of Australia, told certain tales or shown certain scenes, will suddenly be made mad for fucking.[9]

Dutton flounders in his efforts to deal with the complex relations between literature and life and resorts, eventually, to bluster. I have cited him at length since most of the issues I have discussed in previous chapters are threaded through his remarks. The inconsistencies and confusions abound. What are we to make, for example, of his assumption that literature has powerful emotional and persuasive effects on readers – that (good?) literature could (should?) make people mad for laughter, grief, joy, justice, freedom or fucking? How could this be compatible with his claim that literature does not alter people? Undoubtedly propaganda of various kinds (political, commercial, social) can make a suitably pre-disposed audience mad, to varying degrees, for freedom or fascism, soap powders or sex. But good literature is not in direct competition with propaganda. There is no 'message' to be extracted from *Antony and Cleopatra*, or *Voss*. All good literature does, as Dutton says, 'create a world' but it is a *created* world and its relation to our own world is oblique, not directly didactic or simply excitatory of emotion.

When a writer merely moralizes, or merely titillates, 'form' becomes disjunct from 'content' – 'what' is being said is no longer intimately dependent on 'how' it is being said. Abraham Kaplan argues that 'pornography serves to elicit not . . . imaginative contemplation' *of* an experience – 'it is a stimulus to an experience'.[10]

I think that this is partly right but is in need of re-formulation in view of the arguments I put forward in chapters 5 and 6. I distinguished then between (a) works such as tear-jerkers or thrillers in which the *whole point* is to create vicarious emotions in the reader or viewer – to give one a thrill or encourage one to 'have a good cry', and (b) works in which, if such responses are evoked (I cited Hitchcock's best films) they are not evoked for their own sake but form part of the whole orchestrated flow and recoil of sympathy which is characteristic of good literature or film. Pornography is designed to elicit sexual excitement or titillation for its own sake and in this respect it has nothing to do with art, it is mere sensation-seeking. But this is not to say that the arousal of sexual feeling may not be *part* of the enterprise of a good film or work of literature. To return to an example used earlier, in *Fear of Flying* Erica Jong elicits the reader's interest in the details of Isadora's sexual relationships and then confronts the reader with this and 'places' our response. The point remains, however, that one is not just imaginatively contemplating some of the more lurid details of Isadora's life, one does tend to savour them as one might when reading pornography. They are titillatory as are some episodes in a book such as *Fanny Hill*. Kaplan claims that:

When emotions are actually felt (rather than being brought to mind or presented for contemplation) we have overstepped the bounds of art. Sad music does not make us *literally* sad. . . . Of course art evokes feeling, but it is *imagined* feeling, not what is actually felt as a quality of what we do and undergo.[11]

Music presents awkward problems about in what sense, if any, it represents or portrays anything. But in so far as it may be said to portray sadness then it is necessary to say that it may make us *literally* sad, just as a tear-jerker or sob-story may make us literally sad. What we feel in response to representations or portrayals of characters and events is genuine sadness or excitement and what we feel is not imagined feeling. It is the actual experience of feeling sad or excited as a consequence of viewing or reading a portrayal of sad or exciting events or circumstances.

On the account I have offered, good literature never merely stimulates emotion for its own sake, nor does it 'recommend courses of action'; though moral advice or immoral seduction may be 'entertained' they are never, in literature which deals 'seriously' with experience, merely asserted or rejected but rather presented as part of the context of the created 'world' of the work. To invoke Eliot yet again (his comments gain new shades and emphases as they are put in different contexts) the author's 'experience' is 'not an experience in the ordinary sense, for it may only exist, formed out of many personal experiences ordered in some way which may be very different from the way of valuation of practical life, in the expression of it'.[12]

Dealing 'seriously' with experience in literature is incompatible with moralizing and does not mean being solemn. In chapter 1 I referred to Iris Murdoch's comments on 'the playfulness of good art which delightedly seeks and reveals the real . . . of course art is playful, but its play is serious'.[13] Compare Leavis on Marvell: 'Not in the least solemn he is much the more serious.'[14] Murdoch's position has close connections with both Leavis and Arnold:

> [For Leavis and Arnold] there is no *faith* that a serious, mature, intelligent and sincere work of art will ever be wicked as well because such a faith is unnecessary: to call a work with these qualities 'wicked' would just have no sense.[15]

John Casey himself is unable ultimately to accept the position he here attributes to Leavis and Arnold. He wants not to deny the intimate connection between form and content in literary works and in life[16] but finds that 'seriousness', 'intelligence', 'poise', 'sincerity' are compatible with moral badness. A work with these qualities could 'still tell lies about the gods and implicitly or explicitly recommend courses of action which are unwise, superstitious or even wicked'. In Casey's view, Arnold so extends the notion of 'morality' as to make it almost unrecognizable.

Casey's reluctance to cut 'morality in literature' adrift from 'morality' in its usual sense of a code or principles for action (practical reason) is connected with his retention of the notion that a poem can 'tell lies' or 'recommend courses of action or attitude'[17] without degenerating into propaganda or persuasion. Casey's deep concern is that there is a danger that literature may become too decisively cut off from making statements about the world and not really challenge one's beliefs. This is an important concern – there is a sense in which we do want to say that great works of literature have challenged our beliefs, though it is less easy to specify which beliefs have actually *changed* as a result of reading great works of literature.

This is partly because it is particularly difficult in such works to separate out 'the beliefs'. They are present at too complex and concrete a level of enactment, they depend for their existence too intimately on their 'form' – 'these words in these positions'. The 'moral significance', the 'meaning' in great poetry is shifted by an inflection, a slight shift of tone, a pause, a juxtaposition. It is much more likely that our beliefs will be changed by second- or third-rate writing, when it is often closer to propaganda and persuasion.[18]

Casey is worried that if literature is too decisively cut off from making statements about the world we will be cast as elegant aesthetes refusing to attend to what literature 'says' about life. The alternative that he offers, however, is the possibility that we might read or see *Antony and Cleopatra* and 'reject what the play presents in the light of a moral code to which we adhere (or to modify the moral code to which we adhere in the light of what the play presents)'.[19]

There is a crucial tension here for every reader and teacher of literature, between two ultimately unacceptable alternatives, and Casey's book is admirable in its refusal to avoid the tension and adopt a facile solution. My own tendency is to take the risks of some form of aestheticism rather than to allow that a great work of literature, such as *Antony and Cleopatra*, could be viewed in such a way that it (or what it 'presents') could legitimately be rejected in the light of a moral code. To borrow Susanne Langer's phrase, *Antony and Cleopatra* creates a world in which courses of action are 'virtually' recommended and moral positions are 'virtually' adopted and acted out. In chapter 1, I cited Iris Murdoch's observation that literature is 'a great hall of reflection where everything under the sun can be examined and considered'.[20] The nature of this reflection (in both senses of the word) is oblique; different possibilities of experience, feelings, thought, attitudes and actions, in complex interaction are viewed at different angles, from shifting perspectives, in unexpected juxtaposition. Literature cannot reflect life as a mirror does since it is a verbal construction, an ordering, a shaping of characters and words and experience. (Cf. again Eliot's observation that 'the author's experience may only exist in the expression of it'.)

A rather unfair way of dissuading anyone from the direction in which Casey veers (towards literature as a challenge to one's beliefs) and leading in the direction in which I tend (towards a Leavis–Arnold form of 'aestheticism'[21]) is to point out that it becomes more difficult, in Casey's company, to oppose a man such as Mr John Montgomerie, the Chairman of the Working Party of the Arts Council. In his memorandum to the Longford Committee Investigating Pornography in Britain, he argued that 'the balancing of depravity against literary merit is farcical', since 'presumably the better obscenity is written the more it corrupts'.[22] Compare, as well, Mr Justice Duffy, who was certainly prepared to reject a work of literature on moral grounds and who was also prepared to allow that 'literary merit' might enter into his judgement of a work of literature: 'One would suppose that literary skill would make the poison more potent.'[23]

The disconnections for which I have argued between the experience of literature and the experience of life are such that literature is less likely to corrupt or improve us than is often thought. There is a greater gap, I have maintained, between literature and life than is suggested by those who think it will relieve our anxieties and guilts or make us more morally or emotionally refined (when it is 'good' literature) or coarsen us (when it is 'bad' literature). D. H. Lawrence was a passionate advocate of the relevance to life of the novel:

> The novel is the perfect medium for revealing to us the changing rainbow of our living relationships. The novel can help us to live, as nothing else can: no didactic scripture anyhow. If the novelist keeps his thumb out of the pan. But when the novelist has his thumb in the pan (to pull down the balance to his own predilection. . .) the novel becomes an unparalleled perverter of men and women. To be compared only, perhaps, to that great mischief of sentimental hymns, like 'Lead Kindly Light' which have helped to rot the marrow in the bones of the present generation.[24]

I think that this passage is easily misunderstood. The revelation for 'life' that the novel offers is emphatically contrasted with an author's predilections or 'messages'. The revelation is of 'the changing rainbow of our living relationships'. The crucial gap, or disconnection, between the experience of life and the experience of literature for which I have been arguing is reflected in Lawrence's comment that 'Books are not life, they are only tremulations on the ether.' And when he continues by saying that the novel is 'a tremulation which can make the whole man alive tremble'[25] he is not losing sight of the distinctness of literary experience from actual experience because he is contrasting the novel with other '*book* tremulations', such as poetry, philosophy and science.

Despite my insistence on the distinctness of literary experience from the experience of life I was wary, in an earlier chapter, of promoting what David Holbrook refers to as 'the new aestheticism – a split between art and life'.[26] I accept that there is a risk that unless students of literature 'test', in some way, what they read 'against their own experience', literature may become *too* hived off from life and become merely part of a complex game, with the performance of the players adjudicated by teachers in examinations. Against this must be balanced another risk, that what the student 'accepts or rejects' when he tests it against his experience will be a product of a misconception of what the literary experience *is*. He has to be sensitive to the distinctive mode of utterance that literature is. He has to be able to demonstrate a *critical* awareness of the complex ways in which novels and poems 'communicate' experience, if, as T. S. Eliot observes, 'communication is the right word'. When such an awareness *is* possessed it will be apparent to the student that the 'experience' of a literary work is 'not an experience in the ordinary sense'. It will also be apparent that what literary works 'mean' is 'no simple matter' and that testing them against one's own experience runs the continual risk of reducing their 'meaning' to something that can be simply summarized and 'accepted or rejected'.

In cases where good literature is banned or not allowed to reach the shelves of school libraries because of allegedly 'immoral' content, it is particularly important to bring out as strongly as possible the point that is most ignored – the crucial respect in which 'what is said' in good literature is misunderstood if it is separated from its 'form', its context. In this respect literature is not in the domain of assertion, of proposing courses of action, moral or immoral.[27] It may entertain the possibilities of evil and dramatize these possibilities but it does not *advocate* good or evil possibilities. Good literature does not 'compete with moral codes'.

Casey thinks that if literature is to remain in a privileged position 'by refusing to compete with moral codes' the cost is too high. Literature is 'too decisively cut off from forms of expression which make true or false claims about the world'. But even if there is a sense in which literature does 'compete' with such forms of expression it does so in ways that can only with the greatest difficulty be specified. In earlier chapters I have pointed out that coming to grips with the 'meaning' of a good work of literature, to the point where one can claim to have some command of the complex relations between 'parts and whole', is a demanding activity. It is this that needs emphasis in discussions of censorship, particularly in the context of literary education. It is widely assumed by English teachers that literature is just a semi-fictional way of analysing moral and social problems. I referred earlier to the way 'topic-based' courses on 'authority', 'the family' and so on tend to draw on literature as merely a form of social documentary. When literature is thus *forced* to compete by being reduced to 'source material' for social studies or social biology, the costs are very high. To tear the 'thought' out of the delicate 'organic' structure of a work of literature is to destroy it. To do justice to the 'embodied' nature of good literature requires, I have argued, critical skills of the kind I discussed in chapter 2. When the intricate unity of good literature becomes apparent to the critical reader he is less likely to view it as a form of expression reducible to, and thus comparable with, other forms of expression or communication.[28]

In 1969 Philip Roth wrote a letter to the critic Diana Trilling (which he never posted[29]) in which he points out that her review of his novel *Portnoy's Complaint* completely fails to do justice to the novel. Roth denies that he is an 'ideological writer' and he denies that his book is part of what Trilling called 'the latest offensive in our escalating literary-political war against society'.

Obviously I am not looking to be acquitted, as a person, of having some sort of view of things, nor would I hold that my fiction aspires to be a slice of life and nothing more. I am saying only that, as with any novelist, the presentation and the 'position' are inseparable and I don't think a reader would be doing me (or even himself) justice if, for tendentious or polemical purposes, he were to divide the one into two. . .

You describe the book as 'farce with a thesis': yet, when you summarize in a few sentences the philosophical and sociological theses of the novel ('Mr Roth's [book] blames society for the fate we suffer as human individuals and, legitimately or not, invokes Freud on the side of his own grimly deterministic view of life. . .'), not only is much of the book's material pushed over the edge of a cliff to arrive at this conclusion, but there is no indication that the reader's experience of a farce (if that is what you think it is) might work against the grain of the dreary meaning you assign to the book – no indication that the farce might itself be the thesis, if not what you call the 'pedagogic point'. . . May I suggest that perhaps 'Mr Roth's' view of life is more hidden from certain readers . . . than they imagine, more embedded in parody, burlesque, slapstick, ridicule, insult, invective, lampoon, wisecrack, in nonsense, in levity, in *play* – in, that is, the methods and devices of Comedy, than their own view of life may enable them to realise.[30]

Roth claims that in his work virtues and values are 'proposed' as they generally are in fiction – 'largely through the manner of presentation : through what might be called the sensuous aspects of fiction – tone, mood, voice, and among other things, the juxtaposition of the narrative events themselves'.[31]

Roth's letter crisply specifies the ways in which good literature is not in competition with moral codes, is not ideological or pedagogic. The opponents of censorship defend the novelist's or the poet's right to advocate fornication or anything else that takes his fancy. Whereas I have argued throughout this book that good literature is not a form of advocacy, it never simply argues for fornication or fidelity, it does not propose policies at all, moral or immoral. In order to illustrate this I will conclude by considering a poem which the well known critic Donald Davie claims 'overtly advocates fornication'.

To his Coy Mistress

HAD we but World enough, and Time,
This coyness Lady were no crime.
We would sit down, and think which way
To walk, and pass our long Loves Day.
Thou by the *Indian Ganges* side
Should'st Rubies find : I by the Tide
Of *Humber* would complain. I would
Love you ten years before the Flood :
And you should if you please refuse
Till the Conversion of the *Jews*.
My vegetable Love should grow
Vaster then Empires, and more slow.
An hundred years should go to praise
Thine Eyes, and on thy Forehead Gaze.
Two hundred to adore each Breast :
But thirty thousand to the rest.
An Age at least to every part,
And the last Age should show your Heart.
For Lady you deserve this State;
Nor would I love at lower rate.

But at my back I alwaies hear
Times winged Charriot hurrying near:
And yonder all before us lye
Desarts of vast Eternity.
Thy Beauty shall no more be found,
Nor, in thy marble Vault, shall sound
My ecchoing Song: then Worms shall try
That long preserv'd Virginity:
And your quaint Honour turn to dust;
And into ashes all my Lust.
The Grave's a fine and private place,
But none I think do there embrace.
   Now therefore, while the youthful hew
Sits on thy skin like morning dew,
And while thy willing Soul transpires
At every pore with instant Fires,
Now let us sport us while we may;
And now, like am'rous birds of prey,
Rather at once our Time devour,
Than languish in his slow-chapt pow'r.
Let us roll all our Strength, and all
Our sweetness, up into one Ball:
And tear our Pleasures with rough strife,
Thorough the Iron gates of Life.
Thus, though we cannot make our Sun
Stand still, yet we will make him run.

I think it would be grotesque if this poem were defended in the way Dutton defended the tale which allegedly made one 'mad for fucking'. For Marvell's poem does not 'overtly advocate fornication', however integral such advocacy is as part of what is created in the poem.

Donald Davie claims to be unworried by Marvell's 'overt advocacy' despite the fact that his own attitude to fornication is 'different from Marvell's'. He attributes this lack of concern to fact that he has

learnt from Dr Leavis' *Revaluation* how the morality or immorality of a work of literature is hardly at all in what it says ... but in its way of saying it. What we have in Marvell's poems – even in the poem *To his Coy Mistress* which overtly advocates fornication – is a morality by implication, a moral code seen in action in particular human and social situations.[32]

It is not this that I mean by saying that the advocacy of fornication is an integral part of what is created in the poem. For one thing, it is misleading to say that the *poem* advocates fornication. This is what the dramatic speaker is, at one level, proposing to his mistress. I take it that there is an immense difference between saying, 'This poem advocates fornication' and 'This poem presents a lover playfully, seriously, tenderly, mockingly entreating his (probably playfully) coy mistress to make love.'

S. L. Goldberg comments more adequately (on the latter part of the poem) as follows :

> It is characteristic that as the poem drives forward to the consuming act of love, it should keep undiminished all its tenderness, courtesy, understanding, passion and lightness of touch. These values and the act in which they (ironically) seek fulfillment are brought face to face, as it were, but the force of neither kind of vitality is lessened. Once again it is as if the poem, expressing all the values of a subtle, refined consciousness, and its subject, or rather its conclusion – in which those values are necessarily obliterated, were left to measure and complete each other.[33]

The enactment of these values is, of course, intimately a matter of tone, of movement – form and content are fused. Goldberg mentions the way alternatives are measured against each other because they are evoked in terms of each other – the lover's active 'lust' and the worm's, for example, or the present love song (the poem itself) and the silent tomb. 'In fact we hear the song most vividly when it makes us most vividly feel its absence.'

The fact that these points would carry little weight at a trial of Marvell's 'To his Coy Mistress' or with the parents of school children who complain that their children are exposed to literature which advocates fornication makes them no less significant. Furthermore, it is crucial that teachers of literature emphasize the importance of the intricacy and uniqueness of good literature when so many voices, including the 'liberal' voices, defend it for the wrong reasons. Goldberg develops Eliot's view that Marvell's wit is 'a recognition, implicit in the expression of every experience, of other kinds of experience which are possible'. Although he is limiting his remarks to Marvell's poems I think most good literature possesses, in some degree, the characteristics he describes. He denies that Marvell's poems are 'politically or morally indecisive' –

> His subtleties are not a way of avoiding choice and action. But they do delicately insist on the gap between the poet's activities and the activities he is writing about, between their own protean awareness and the limiting action forced on us in ordinary life.[34] In other words, although the poetry continually judges the experience it evokes it never purports

actually to settle anything. It claims no didactic or ideological usefulness. It offers itself only as an example . . . living with irreconcilable conflicts easily, finely and without losing one's head.[35]

It is a matter of considerable critical delicacy to insist on the gap between the poet's activities and the activities he is writing about. But unless this gap is maintained the study of literature becomes merely the servant of other pursuits. Literature has a distinctive voice in 'the conversation of mankind' and if its manner of illuminating experience is reduced to that of other disciplines or forms of discourse it will not be audible. The central task of literary education is to alert students to the unique characteristics of this mode of utterance.

Notes

Introduction

1. John Casey, *The Language of Criticism* (London, Methuen, 1966).
2. Denis Donoghue (Henry James Professor of Letters at New York University) has recently commented: 'No one's heart is likely to be stirred by the thought of holding a conference on the question of What it Means to Teach English in the University. But I have no doubt that the issues of such a conference have been silently set aside as too boring or too distasteful to be raised: they have not been resolved' (*T.L.S.* (6 Feb. 1981), 136). On the other hand there are some welcome new developments such as the 'Critical Forum' section of *Essays in Criticism* which is mainly devoted to raising questions about the nature of criticism.

1. *Literature and truth*

1. Erica Jong, *Fear of Flying* (London, Granada, 1974), pp. 169–70.
2. Iris Murdoch, *The Fire and the Sun* (Oxford, Clarendon Press, 1977), pp. 65–6.
3. *Ibid.* p. 72.
4. Iris Murdoch, *The Flight from the Enchanter* (London, Penguin, 1962), pp. 122–3.
5. *The Fire and the Sun*, p. 80.
6. *Fear of Flying*, p. 194. This is a version of W. H. Auden's question, 'How do I know what I think till I see what I say?'
7. Probably the most common way of establishing that something is potentially educative is that it leads to knowledge and understanding – history and science develop knowledge and understanding of the past and of the physical world, for example. Astrology and alchemy are not educative, however, because they do not lead to knowledge and understanding. (Though we could have knowledge *about* and understanding *of* alchemy and astrology as part of the history of ideas, and *this* could be educative.)
8. First published in *Philosophical Review*, vol. 54 (1945). Republished in many anthologies.
9. Monroe Beardsley, *Aesthetics* (New York, Harcourt, Brace and World, 1958), p. 410.
10. The 'logical puzzle' is apparently a consequence of Beardsley's belief that all concepts must have actual application in the observable world to be meaningful.
11. A. Isenberg, 'The problem of belief', *Contemporary Studies in Aesthetics*, ed. J. Francis Coleman (New York, McGraw-Hill, 1968), p. 260; Bertram Jessup, 'On fictional expressions of cognitive meaning', *Journal of Aesthetic and Art Criticism*, vol. 23, no. 4 (Summer 1965), 486; Beardsley, *Aesthetics*, p. 410.

12. Jerome Stolnitz, *Aesthetics and the Philosophy of Art Criticism* (New York, Houghton Mifflin, 1960), pp. 325–6.
13. Morris Weitz, 'Truth in Literature', *Introductory Readings in Aesthetics*, ed. John Hospers (New York, Free Press, 1969), p. 233.
14. *Ibid.* p. 215. But, as Paul Hirst points out, 'there is a perfectly good concept of a mermaid, though no mermaids exist'. A more recent example (among many) of preoccupation with this 'puzzle' is 'Truth in fiction', David Lewis, *American Philosophical Quarterly*, vol. 15, no. 1 (Jan. 1978). At least Lewis is explicit that he is not concerned with appreciation of fiction or critical insight.
15. R. K. Elliott, 'The aesthetic and the semantic', *The British Journal of Aesthetics*, vol. 8, no. 1 (Jan. 1968).
16. *The Fire and the Sun*, pp. 83–6.
17. Matthew Arnold, *The Study of Poetry* in *Matthew Arnold*, ed. John Bryson (Cambridge, Mass., Harvard University Press, 1970), p. 671.
18. John Casey, *The Language of Criticism* (London, Methuen, 1966), p. 180.
19. There is an inescapable air of paradox in commenting on these lines, of course. Am I joining the company of the despised critics, Kuster, Burman and Wasse? Presumably this would be so only if I make the same kinds of mistake in my analysis as they do in theirs.
20. L. Wittgenstein, *Philosophical Investigations* (Oxford, Blackwell, 1967), para. 531.
21. *Ibid.*, paras. 531–3.
22. D. W. Harding, *Experience into Words* (London, Chatto and Windus, 1970), p. 99.
23. *Ibid.* pp. 109–10.
24. In his marginalia on *Romeo and Juliet*, Coleridge distinguishes Shakespeare's 'creative power' from 'mechanical talent' for which 'each part is separately conceived and then by a succeeding act put together'. *Coleridge's Shakespearian Criticism*, ed. T. M. Raysor (London, Constable, 1930), vol. 1, p. 4.
25. In *Four Quartets* T. S. Eliot dramatizes the difficulty which many writers report, of the struggle to 'get it right', e.g.:

> Words strain,
> Crack and sometimes break, under the burden,
> Under the tension, slip, slide, perish,
> Decay with imprecision, will not stay in place,
> Will not stay still.

26. *Experience into Words*, p. 187.
27. *Ibid.* p. 172 (my italics).
28. See, however, chapter 7 below, 'Literary intention and literary education'.
29. I have adopted inverted commas for the term 'experience' since I do not want to beg any questions about its meaning. Not only is there Harding's point that we must not assume that 'experience' is at any stage independent of words, that words play a part in shaping the nature of experience. There is also a question about what con-

stitutes the 'reality' of an experience, especially when we refer to a literary artist's communication or 'expression' of an experience. T. S. Eliot has some significant points to make about this which I will turn to in a moment.

30. *Experience into Words*, pp. 170–1.

31. *Ibid.* p. 171.

32. Cf. E. M. W. Tillyard's reference to the 'old truth' that 'the greatest things in literature are the most commonplace': *The Elizabethan World Picture* (London, Chatto and Windus, 1967), p. 101.

33. T. S. Eliot, *The Use of Poetry and the Use of Criticism* (London, Faber, 1933), p. 130 (my italics). Cf. A. C. Bradley:

> for poetry's nature is to be not a part, nor yet a copy, of the real world (as we commonly understand that phrase), but to be a world by itself, independent, complete, autonomous; and to possess it fully you must enter that world, conform to its laws, and ignore for the time the beliefs, aims and particular conditions which belong to you in the other world of reality. . . There is plenty of connection between life and poetry but it is, so to say, a connection underground. . . . we understand one by help of the other, and even, in a sense, care for one because of the other: but . . . poetry neither is life, nor, strictly speaking, a copy of it . . . they have different *kinds* of existence ('Poetry for poetry's sake', *Oxford Lectures on Poetry* (London, Macmillan, 1959), pp. 5–6).

34. Consider, for example, the following introduction and poem written by Jennifer, aged 13.

Mickey

For a few short years, I had a friend more loving and true to me than anyone I can ever hope to meet again.

But Mickey, though he was true and loving, was not the type of dog who could be satisfied with a single walk a day. Thus it was that I sadly parted with him, happy only in that I knew he now may run all day without any danger; in the countryside which was to become his home.

It was then, to achieve relief from the pain of his departure, that I wrote a lament, for which these words serve only as an introduction.

A Lament to Mickey

I cannot help my lips to breathe one sigh,
Nor the tears that gently fill my eye,
For though I am so happy and so glad,
As I think of him my heart is sad –
He does not need me any more,
That is the past, that was before,
When he slept in his old, dear, smelly chair,
That's when he loved me so very much,
When he'd cheer me with his loving touch.
Smack him, and you'd get a lick,
O Mick – my darling, loyal Mick.
That Mick and I are so far apart
Shall never cease to hurt my heart.
To me he was so faithful, so divine
That I'll always think of him as mine,
. . . Long after he's forgotten me.

Professor James Britton comments on his example as follows:

A very unpolished piece of literature. Judging from outside, we might say that had the words more sharply fitted the experience, the process of coming to terms with it would have been more effective.

Britton assumes that Jennifer is trying to 'fit' her words to an 'experience' which pre-dates the poem. Whereas I would argue that Jennifer is taking the experience as the *occasion* to compose a lament. I think it would be a mistake to encourage the child to try to find words which more accurately described her feelings towards her pet. She is trying to *dramatize* her feelings by composing a lament. One of the major difficulties she has in achieving this is the rhyme-scheme she employs. It would free her poetic imagination, her inventiveness, if she did not feel obliged to find words to fit the rhyme. But she would be freed to *make* something real rather than to accurately recall a real experience (James Britton, 'Literature' in *The Arts in Education* (London, Evans, 1963), p. 47).

2. *Literary criticism and literary education*

1. L. A. Reid, *Meaning in the Arts* (London, Allen and Unwin, 1969), p. 217.
2. P. H. Hirst, 'Literature and the fine arts as a unique form of knowledge', *Knowledge and the Curriculum* (London, Routledge and Kegan Paul, 1974), p. 161.
3. *Meaning in the Arts*, p. 217.
4. 'Literature and the fine arts', p. 163.
5. J. Stolnitz, *Aesthetics and the Philosophy of Art Criticism* (New York, Houghton Mifflin, 1960).
6. John White, *Towards a Compulsory Curriculum* (London, Routledge and Kegan Paul, 1973), p. 28.
7. F. R. Leavis, *Education and the University* (London, Chatto and Windus, 1943), p. 71.
8. A. C. Bradley, *Oxford Lectures on Poetry* (London, Macmillan, 1959), p. 19.
9. Sonia Greger, 'Aesthetic meaning', *Proc. of the Phil. of Education Soc. of G. B.* Supp. Issue, vol. 6, no. 2 (1972), 148–9.
10. T. S. Eliot, *Selected Essays* (London, Faber and Faber, 1932), p. 300.
11. 'Aesthetic meaning', p. 149.
12. F. R. Leavis, *The Living Principle* (London, Chatto and Windus, 1975), pp. 89–90. (Leavis' analysis is cited below, pp. 49–50.)
13. *Education and the University*, p. 77.
14. S. T. Coleridge, *Biographia Literaria*, ed. J. Shawcross (Oxford University Press, 1907), vol. II, p. 12.
15. I have not considered an argument which is sometimes hinted at by the opponents of literary criticism in education concerning the alleged 'subjectivity' of criticism. Since education involves a concern for objectivity of judgement there are some important questions here, though I have never seen them adequately discussed. I will try to tackle some of them in chapter 3.
16. *Meaning in the Arts*, p. 224.

17. Or of our misapprehension or misunderstanding, of course.
18. Diane Collinson, *New Essays in the Philosophy of Education*, ed. G. Langford and D. J. O'Connor (London, Routledge and Kegan Paul, 1973), p. 205.
19. *Ibid.* p. 205.
20. Cf. R. S. Peters' analysis in *Ethics and Education* (London, Allen and Unwin, 1966). Also C. K. Harris, 'Peters on Schooling', *Educational Philosophy and Theory*, vol. 9, no. 1 (1977).
21. In his essay 'Reality and sincerity', Leavis refers to the majority of readers who do not think Hardy's poem 'After a Journey' to be superior to Emily Brontë's 'Cold in the Earth'. As one of this majority I was sceptical of Leavis' claim that, 'for such readers, the superiority can be demonstrated; that is, established to their satisfaction'. However I found myself unable to resist the telling appropriateness of such comments as the following, on 'Cold in the Earth': 'Emily Brontë conceives a situation in order to have the satisfaction of a disciplined imaginative exercise: the satisfaction of dramatizing herself in a tragic role – an attitude, nobly impressive, of sternly controlled passionate desolation' (*The Living Principle*, p. 129).
22. For some reservations about this potentially misleading term see A. Kettle, *An Introduction to the English Novel*, vol. 1 (London, Hutchinson, 1959), p. 18.
23. Henry James, 'The art of fiction', *The House of Fiction*, ed. Leon Edel (London, Hart-Davis, 1957), p. 34.
24. *Ibid.* p. 39.
25. I cited as an example of such a 'dead' passage the description Isadora offers of peeling off various masks of dishonesty, none of which is sufficiently distinguishable from the other to be separated. The failure of the 'expression' *is* a failure of the 'thought'.
26. *An Introduction to the English Novel*, pp. 130 and 132.
27. *Ibid.* p. 132.
28. *Ibid.* p. 123.
29. Norman Page, *The Language of Jane Austen* (Oxford University Press, 1972), pp. 48–53 and 127–36.
30. A. Walton Litz, '*Persuasion*: "forms of estrangement"'' in *Northanger Abbey and Persuasion, a Casebook,* ed. B. C. Southam (London, Macmillan, 1976).
31. See p. 25 above for some comments on literary 'devices'.
32. Bradbury expands this as follows: 'Anne, originally persuaded towards a certain caution appropriate to rank and security, comes to question the values associated with these for those of energetic uncertainty and promise.'
33. *Northanger Abbey and Persuasion, a Casebook*, p. 223.
34. *Education and the University*, p. 76.
35. *Ibid.* p. 70.
36. Forty years ago Leavis pointed out the inadequacies of the 'measuring with a norm' 'one-eye-on-the-standard' approach to criticism as it was then argued by the philosopher Rene Wellek (*Scrutiny*, vol.

6 (1936), 59–70). It makes no difference to Wellek's philosophical descendants, however:

> The critic must be able to state clearly what he means by 'beauty' or 'greatness' in art. He must make explicit the criteria or yardsticks of value in the light of which he arrived at his judgement. If he fails to do this his criticism is hopelessly vague and we literally do not know what he is talking about.
>
> (Jerome Stolnitz, *Aesthetics and the Philosophy of Art Criticism*)

For my own rebuttal of this position, see pp. 63–76 below.

37. *Education and the University*, p. 78.
38. The reader is advised to have at hand a copy of *The Living Principle*, which contains these essays and also the texts of the poems to be discussed.
39. *The Living Principle*, pp. 89–90.
40. *Revaluation* (London, Chatto and Windus, 1962), p. 263.
41. *Ibid.* pp. 263–4.
42. *The Living Principle*, p. 93.
43. *Ibid.* pp. 71–93.
44. *Ibid.* p. 78.
45. *Ibid.* p. 81.
46. *Ibid.* p. 86.
47. *Ibid.* pp. 86–7.
48. 'The enactment fallacy', *Essays in Criticism*, vol. 30, no. 2 (Apr. 1980), 95.
49. *Ibid.* p. 103.
50. *Ibid.* p. 103.
51. *The Living Principle*, p. 111.
52. *Education and the University*, pp. 76–8.
53. See above, pp. 37–8.
54. *Education and the University*, p. 78.
55. *The Living Principle*, pp. 110–11.
56. See above, pp. 29–30.
57. *The Living Principle*, p. 134.
58. 'The motivation of Tennyson's weeper' in *Critical Essays on the Poetry of Tennyson*, ed. John Killham (London, Routledge, 1960), p. 182.
59. *Ibid.* p. 180.
60. *Ibid.* p. 190.
61. *Ibid.* p. 190.
62. *Ibid.* pp. 190–1.
63. *The Living Principle*, pp. 110–11.
64. M. Oakeshott, 'The voice of poetry in the conversation of mankind' in *Rationalism in Politics* (London, Methuen, 1962).

3. Objectivity and subjectivity in literary education

1. Margaret Macdonald, 'Some distinctive features of arguments used in criticism of the arts' in *Aesthetics and Language*, ed. W. Elton (Oxford, Blackwell, 1954), p. 130.

2. *Ibid.* p. 129.
3. John Casey, *The Language of Criticism* (London, Methuen, 1966), p. 174.
4. S. Toulmin, *Human Understanding*, vol. I (Oxford, Clarendon Press, 1972), p. 171.
5. D. H. Monro, *Empiricism and Ethics* (Cambridge University Press, 1967), p. 18.
6. L. Wittgenstein, *On Certainty*, ed. G. M. Anscombe and G. H. von Wright (Oxford, Blackwell, 1969).
7. F. N. Sibley and M. Tanner, 'Objectivity and aesthetics', *Proc. of the Aristotelian Soc.*, Supp., vol. 42 (1968), 36.
8. *Ibid.* p. 42.
9. Michael Scriven, 'The objectivity of aesthetic evaluation', *The Monist*, vol. 50, no. 2 (Apr. 1966), 180.
10. *Ibid.* p. 165.
11. *Ibid.* p. 180.
12. John Wilson, 'Education and aesthetic appreciation: a review', *Oxford Review of Education*, vol. 3, no. 2 (1977), 199.
13. Wilson acknowledges that someone may see the move as neat, elegant, economical – i.e. efficient – but still not warm to the move *in the way* that a person who loved chess as an art form would warm to it.
14. 'Education and aesthetic appreciation', p. 199.
15. E.g. Renford Bambrough, Peter Byrne, Richard Schusterman, John Casey.
16. Peter Byrne, 'Leavis, literary criticism and philosophy', *British Journal of Aesthetics*, vol. 19, no. 3 (Summer 1979), 268.
17. *Ibid.* p. 266.
18. Richard Peacock, *Criticism and Personal Taste* (Oxford, Clarendon Press, 1972), p. 124.
19. *The Language of Criticism*, p. 169.
20. David Hume, *A Treatise of Human Nature* in *Hume's Ethical Writings*, ed. Alisdair MacIntyre (New York and London, Collier Books, Macmillan, 1965), pp. 195 and 180.
21. Hugo Meynell, 'The objectivity of value judgements', *Philosophical Quarterly*, no. 21 (1971), 123.
22. *Criticism and Personal Taste*, p. 26.
23. *Ibid.* p. 35.
24. *Ibid.* p. 23.
25. *Ibid.* p. 9.
26. 'Leavis, literary criticism and philosophy', p. 271.

4. *The subordination of criticism to theory*

1. Jonathan Culler, *Structuralist Poetics* (London, Routledge and Kegan Paul, 1975), p. vii.
2. *Ibid.* p. 255.
3. *Ibid.* p. viii.

4. *Ibid.* p. viii.
5. *Ibid.* p. viii.
6. *Ibid.* p. 75.
7. *Ibid.* p. 166.
8. *Ibid.* p. 119.
9. *Ibid.* p. 122.
10. *Ibid.* p. 245.
11. *Ibid.* p. 247.
12. *Ibid.* pp. 250–1.
13. *Ibid.* p. 251.
14. *Ibid.* p. 251.
15. *Ibid.* p. 253.
16. *Ibid.* p. 244.
17. *Ibid.* p. 118.
18. *Ibid.* p. 187.
19. *Ibid.* p. 117.
20. *Ibid.* p. 247.
21. *Ibid.* p. 132.
22. *Ibid.* p. 130.
23. *Ibid.* p. 259.
24. *Ibid.* p. 259.
25. *Ibid.* p. 261.
26. *Ibid.* p. 261.
27. *Ibid.* p. 261.
28. *Ibid.* p. 261.
29. Harold Bloom *et al.*, *Deconstruction and Criticism* (London, Routledge and Kegan Paul, 1979), p. 14.
30. *Ibid.* p. 14.
31. *Ibid.* pp. 14–15.
32. *Ibid.* p. 249.
33. *Ibid.* pp. 252–3.
34. 'The deconstruction gang', *London Review of Books* (22 May–4 Jun. 1980), 15.
35. 'In theory', *London Review of Books* (16 Apr.–6 May 1981), 6.
36. Terence Hawkes, *Structuralism and Semiotics* (London, Methuen, 1977), pp. 156–7.
37. A note left on a kitchen table which read 'This is just to say I have eaten the plums which were in the icebox and which you were probably saving for breakfast. Forgive me, they were delicious : so sweet and so cold' would be a nice gesture; but when it is set down on the page as a poem the convention of significance comes into play. We deprive the poem of the pragmatic and circumstantial functions of the note (retaining simply this reference to a context as an implicit assertion that this sort of experience is important), and we must therefore supply a new function to justify the poem. Given the opposition between the eating of plums and the social rules which this violates, we may say that the poem as note becomes the mediating force, recognizing the priority of rules by asking forgiveness but also affirming, by the thrust of the last few words, that immediate sensuous experience also has its claims and that the order of personal relations (the relationship between the 'I' and the 'you') must

make a place for such experience. We can go on from there and say that the world of notes and breakfast is also the world of language, which cannot assimilate or stand up to these moments when, as Valery says, 'le fruit se fonde en jouissance'. The value affirmed by the eating of plums is something that transcends language and cannot be captured by the poem except negatively (as apparent insignificance), which is why the poem must be so sparse and superficially banal.

(*Structuralist Poetics*, pp. 175–6)

38. *Structuralism and Semiotics*, pp. 139–40.
39. *The Modes of Modern Writing* (London, Edward Arnold, 1977), p. 52.
40. *Ibid.* p. 123.
41. David Lodge, *Working with Structuralism* (London, Routledge and Kegan Paul, 1981).
42. *Ibid.* pp. 108–9.
43. *Ibid.* pp. 107–8.
44. *Ibid.* p. 21.

5. Literature and the education of the emotions

1. Raymond Wilson, 'Literature' in *Values and Evaluation in Education*, ed. Roger Straughan and Jack Wrigley (London, Harper and Row, 1980), p. 138.
2. B. S. Bloom *et al.*, *Taxonomy of Educational Objectives. The Classification of Educational Goals. Handbook I, The Cognitive Domain* (London, Longmans Green, 1956), *Handbook II, The Affective Domain* (London, Longmans Green, 1964). For ease of reference I refer to Bloom without mentioning the names of his colleagues.
3. 'English past, present and future' in *New Movements in the Study and Teaching of English* (London, Temple Smith, 1973), p. 46.
4. *Taxonomy, Handbook II*, p. 56.
5. Rudolf Carnap, *Philosophy and Logical Syntax* (London, Psyche miniatures, gen. ser. 20, 1935), p. 28.
6. *Taxonomy, Handbook II*, p. 43.
7. See my *Introduction to Philosophy of Education* (Boston, Allyn and Bacon, 1969), pp. 29–40.
8. *Taxonomy, Handbook II*, p. 53.
9. There are some very awkward questions to be considered concerning the *nature* of the emotional response. What connections are there between the emotions which are appropriate to seeing a performance of *King Lear* and those which are occasioned by perceptions of events in the real world? If we expect students to be 'moved' by works of literature, *what* do we expect? And what could we legitimately expect? I will tackle each of these questions in the remainder of this chapter and in the following chapter.
10. R. S. Peters and C. A. Mace, 'Emotions and the category of passivity', *Proceedings of the Aristotelian Society* (Jan. 1962), 139. Cf. more recently, Jerry L. Guthrie puts forward as an 'uncontroversial assumption' that 'emotional response to an "object" presupposes

some belief (true or false) about the object of response'. 'Self-deception and emotional response to fiction', *The British Journal of Aesthetics*, vol. 21 (1981), 66.

11. *Taxonomy, Handbook II*, pp. 55–6.
12. William Hare argues that establishing that x enjoys y does not establish that x appreciates y 'for this will be denied if others judge that x provides irrelevant, inappropriate or generally unacceptable reasons to support his judgement. It makes good sense to say that x does not appreciate *King Lear* if he thinks of it as a comedy' ('Appreciation as a goal of aesthetic education', *The Journal of Aesthetic Education*, vol. 8, no. 2 (Apr. 1974).
13. *Taxonomy, Handbook I*, p. 198.
14. *The Common Pursuit* (London, Chatto and Windus, 1962), p. 213.
15. Susanne Langer, *Feeling and Form* (London, Routledge, 1953), p. 262. For an excellent example of how apparent capriciousness and fragmentation are made significant in art, see Robin Wood's account of the shower murder in Hitchcock's *Psycho*, note 20 below.
16. H. O. Mounce, 'Art and real life', *Philosophy*, vol. 55, no. 212 (Apr. 1980), 188.
17. *Ibid.* pp. 191–2.
18. Colin Radford and Michael Weston, 'How can we be moved by the fate of Anna Karenina?' *P.A.S.*, Supp., vol. 49 (1975), 67–93.
19. Robin Wood, *Hitchcock's Films* (London and New York, Zwemmer, 1965).
20. Wood's book is thick with examples, but here is his account of the significance of the famous shower murder:

> Consider the totally arbitrary and pointless nature of the shower murder in *Psycho* from the point of view of Marion and her development at that point. From her point of view – which is after all that from which we have been watching the film – the murder has no dramatic, symbolic or thematic justification. If she were still in her compulsive state, if she had not just been released from it and made her free decision to return the money, the murder could be taken as having some validity as retribution (though grossly disproportionate) or as a symbolic representation of the irrevocability of her descent into the chaos-world. But Marion is saved. It is partly because the murder is – again from her point of view – entirely arbitrary and unpredictable that its effect is so shattering. We are made to feel at that moment the precariousness, the utter unreasonableness of life.
>
> (*Hitchcock's Films*, p. 116)

21. 'Art and real life', p. 190.
22. 'The fate of Anna Karenina', pp. 92–3.
23. David Holbrook, *The Exploring Word* (Cambridge University Press, 1967), p. 81.
24. Frank Whitehead *et al.*, *Children and their Books* (London, Macmillan, 1977).
25. See, for example, *ibid.* pp. 208 and 252.
26. *Ibid.* p. 210.
27. *Ibid.* p. 224.

28. *Ibid.* p. 224.
29. *Ibid.* p. 224.
30. *Ibid.* p. 225.
31. *Ibid.* p. 219.
32. David Hume, 'On Tragedy', *Hume's Essays* (Oxford University Press, 1963), p. 221.
33. Cited in David Daiches, *Critical Approaches to Literature* (London, Longman, 1963), p. 160.

6. *Empathy and literary education*

1. Frank Whitehead *et al.*, *Children and their Books* (London, Macmillan, 1977), pp. 222–3.
2. The Schools Council authors acknowledge this later (pp. 225–6) but fail to see its incompatibility with their preceding analysis.
3. *Children and their Books*, p. 222.
4. It is not apparent to me what we are to make of the suggestion that in *The Secret Agent* the reader's main emotional satisfaction is that of joining with Conrad in his authorial evaluative judgement of Mr. Verloc. I can only assume that the Schools Council authors find *The Secret Agent* to be a kind of *exception* to their generalization that the reader's emotional response is essentially a matter of wish-fulfilment. They surely can't mean that the reader wishes to be Conrad!
5. See above, pp. 101–2.
6. *The Plowden Report*, cited in *Towards a New English*, ed. A. Ashworth and K. Watson (Sydney, Reed, 1972).
7. See, for example, Ernst Nagel, *The Structure of Science* (New York, Harcourt Brace, 1961); Karl Hempel, 'The function of general laws in history', *Journal of Philosophy*, vol. 39 (Jan. 1942); Peter Winch, *The Idea of a Social Science* (London, Routledge and Kegan Paul, 1958); W. H. Dray, *Laws and Explanation in History* (Oxford University Press, 1957); J. B. Hunsdahl, 'Concerning Einfühlung (empathy): a concept analysis of its origin and early development', *Journal of the History of Behavioural Sciences*, vol. 3, no. 2 (1967). I discuss some aspects of the work of each of these writers in 'Empathy and education', *Studies in Philosophy and Education*, vol. 8, no. 1 (Summer 1973), written in conjunction with Graham Oliver. Some of the material in this section of the present chapter is drawn from this paper and I wish to express my indebtedness to Oliver for the ideas I have borrowed.
8. Patrick Creber, *Sense and Sensitivity* (University of London Press, 1965), p. 19.
9. 'Justifying curriculum decisions' in *Philosophical Essays on Teaching*, ed. B. Bandman and R. Guttchen (Philadelphia, Lippincott, 1967).
10. *The Theory of Knowledge* (London, Macmillan, 1970), pp. 104–6.
11. *Ibid.* p. 124.

12. Hamlyn's discussion of knowledge of other persons, like my own, ignores the traditional philosophical problems associated with 'knowledge of other minds'. As Hamlyn points out, 'once given that we are confronted with a person, the existence of another mind is not problematic' (*ibid.* p. 240).

13. *Ibid.* p. 247.

14. *Explaining, Understanding and Teaching* (New York, McGraw-Hill, 1970), p. 144.

15. *Ibid.* p. 182.

16. For the distinction between 'task' and 'achievement' verbs see Gilbert Ryle, *The Concept of Mind* (Harmondsworth, Penguin, 1963), pp. 130 and 150–3. For a brief comment on the distinction see my *Introduction to Philosophy of Education* (Boston, Allyn and Bacon, 1969), p. 5. There are some obscurities in the distinction, noted by I. Scheffler, *Conditions of Knowledge* (Scott, Foresman, Glenview, Ill., 1965), p. 33.

17. 'Sympathy' seems to be closely related to Martin's 'being understanding'. Martin refers to both 'sympathy' and 'empathy' without attending to the differences between these two concepts. In my view, 'sympathy' implies 'feeling for' an agent and 'empathy' implies 'feeling with' an agent. Sympathizing with someone means knowing how he feels and caring how he feels. Empathizing, on the other hand, means knowing how he feels and feeling the same sort of feeling with him. In empathizing, 'caring how he feels' is implicit in one's own affective response – to the extent that you feel the way he feels you 'care' for him as you care for yourself. The important point is that you could care for him *without* feeling the way he feels. If this were so we would describe this as sympathy.

Martin receives some support from the *O.E.D.*, which includes the following definitions: 'the quality or state of being affected by the condition of another with a feeling similar or corresponding to that of the other; the fact or capacity of entering into or sharing the feelings of another or others'. However, I would contend that in ordinary usage 'sympathy' has come to mean something very close to 'pity' or 'feeling sorry for'. It is odd to claim to feel sympathy for another's happiness, pleasure, triumph, success, pride, jealousy, etc. A condition of feeling sympathy for X is that X is suffering or in distress of some sort. But even in this much more limited context it is not necessary to 'enter into' or 'share the feelings' of X in order to sympathize with X. We may find X's dog to be a revolting animal and may feel none of X's grief over its death but still feel sympathy towards X. Furthermore, we may be quite unable to see the death of a dog as being a reason for grief but still feel sympathy towards X simply because he is suffering. It is not necessary to see why X suffers in order to sympathize with him. All that is necessary is to perceive that he does suffer. In what follows, I argue that empathy requires that the observer see in the situation sufficient reason for the person to feel as he does if he is to empathize with him.

18. I have already acknowledged Graham Oliver's extensive contribution to the ideas advanced in this section. This example and the following one are his suggestions.

19. The point is Graham Oliver's and his examples are worth citing:

> It is not necessary that the observer be afraid of mice to see that the woman standing on the chair has reason to fear them. Knowing that normal people often are scared of mice; recognizing qualities of movement and size which some people might find unsettling; remembering similar irrational fears such as fear of spiders, worms or snakes – even when such fears have been overcome – may serve to permit even the mouselover to understand that mice could be seen as a reason to be afraid. The aborigine who sees the white man turning pale when offered a grub to eat may be unable to see that a man could react in this way to such a delicacy.

20. R. Heilman, *The Ghost on the Ramparts* (Athens, Ga., University of Georgia Press, 1973).

21. *Ibid.* p. 21.

22. *Ibid.* p. 24.

23. *Ibid.* p. 26

24. Throughout the poem the imagery employed by the speaker in his attempts to define his own nothingness has implied the possibility of new life and hope – the alchemical imagery, for example, and the chaos from which the world began. As the speaker casts around desperately to define his total absence of identity he realizes where *his* sun will rise – in the next life. And the realization occurs between stanzas 4 and 5. Stanza 5 is calm, assured and strongly assertive of identity and being – it must be the only poem in the language to finish on the word 'is'. 'For this both the year's and the day's deep midnight is'.

25. Rosamond Tuve, *Elizabethan and Metaphysical Imagery* (University of Chicago Press, 1947). See ch. 9, section 2, for Tuve's account of 'ironia'.

26. John F. Danby, *Elizabethan and Jacobean Poets* (London, Faber and Faber, 1952), p. 135.

7. *Literary intention and literary education*

1. W. K. Wimsatt and Monroe C. Beardsley, 'The intentional fallacy', *The Verbal Icon* (University of Kentucky Press, 1954).

2. Boswell, *Life of Johnson*, 9 Apr. 1777, cited in W. K. Wimsatt, 'Genesis: a fallacy re-visited' and in F. Cioffi, 'Intention and interpretation in criticism'. Both essays appear in *On Literary Intention*, ed. D. Newton-de Molina (Edinburgh University Press, 1976).

3. *Goldsmith* (1848) I, 369, cited in *On Literary Intention*.

4. D. W. Harding, *Experience into Words* (London, Chatto and Windus, 1970), p. 164.

5. 'You have to remember that *Psycho* is a film made with quite a sense of amusement on my part. To me it is a *fun* picture. The processes through which we take the audience, you see, it's rather

like taking them through the haunted house at the fairground. . .'
(extract from an interview with Alfred Hitchcock cited in Robin
Wood, *Hitchcock's Films* (London and New York, Zwemmer, 1965),
p. 114.

6. *Ibid.*

7. That this seems to be a melodramatic exaggeration on Wood's part
is beside the present point.

8. There is some evidence that Hitchcock plays games with his inter-
viewers. When asked why James Mason's supposed wife in *North
by Northwest* comes in to ask her husband to receive guests who
don't seem to exist, he responded, 'I know nothing about it. I don't
know the lady in question. I've never met her. I don't know why
she came in then or why she said that.'

9. 'Intention and interpretation in criticism', p. 66.

10. In section (b) I will argue that in Cioffi's critical practice this conception of 'biographical reference' allows too much weight to be
given to authors' statements of their generative intention at the
expense of what is (operatively) realized in their work.

11. For example, at the end of the film a psychiatrist drones on
simplistically and portentously about Norman Bates' (the murder-
er's) psychopathology. Behind the psychiatrist's head in the
police station hangs a picture of a police motor cycle stuntman.
The mocking rhyming slang for psychiatrist is 'trick cyclist'.
Pictures on the wall in Hitchcock's films characteristically relate to
what is taking place in the foreground. Is Hitchcock intending to
poke fun at the psychiatrist? I think so, though even here it's not
just poking fun. It is part of the glib and superficial pretension of
the psychiatrist, the exposure of which is, in turn, part of the very
serious purpose in the film.

12. 'The literary past' in *On Literary Intention*, p. 165.

13. *The Use of Poetry and the Use of Criticism* (London, Faber and
Faber, 1933), p. 30 (my italics).

14. 'Intention and interpretation in criticism'.

15.   Let us roll all our Strength, and all
                    Our sweetness, up into one Ball:
                    And tear our Pleasures with rough strife,
                    Thorough the Iron gates of Life.

16. 'Intention and interpretation in criticism', p. 60.

17. If Yeats later came to prefer 'Soldier' this does not, of course, show
that he could have meant 'Soldier' when he wrote 'Solider'.

18. I had not originally intended (so to speak!) to deal so exhaustively
with Cioffi's examples. I thought that Cioffi had gone astray at a
few crucial points and that these reflected the pitfalls into which
non-philosophers (teachers/students) could more easily fall if they
attempted to follow in Cioffi's footsteps. However, a sturdy defender
of Cioffi argued that I had misunderstood his position and neglected
his most telling examples. Whether or not my attempt to dispose
of each of Cioffi's examples succeeds I want to acknowledge my debt
to the critic who insisted that I should at least try to do justice to

Cioffi's paper. In the course of wrestling with Cioffi I have also tried out my ideas on my colleague, Dr. Martin Bibby. While I remain unconvinced that my arguments are wrong, he has made me aware that I have a lot more thinking to do.

19. E. F. Sparshott, 'Criticism and performance' in *On Literary Intention*, p. 105.
20. 'Intention and critical judgement', *Essays in Criticism*, vol. 25, no. 2 (Apr. 1975), 219.

8. *Literature, morality and censorship*

1. I am grateful to Jo Karaolis for drawing my attention to this passage.
2. *Pornography: the Longford Report* (London, Coronet Books, 1972), p. 451.
3. *Lady Chatterley's Lover* was banned in Australia after its release by the English jury's verdict. C. H. Rolph's book reporting the trial was also banned in Australia. (Cf. *Moll Flanders* released in 1937, *A Farewell to Arms, Brave New World* and *Ulysses* in 1938. In the 1950s *Catcher in the Rye, Lolita* and *Borstal Boy* were to be banned.)
4. In 1923 the British Customs banned and burnt all but one copy of an edition of 500 copies. It was released in 1937. The American Customs banned *Ulysses* in 1922 but released it in 1933. It is worth noting that as recently as 1932 a poet who had translated some coarse poems by Rabelais and a parody of Verlaine was sentenced to six months' imprisonment which he served in Wormwood Scrubs prison. Count de Montalk left his manuscript with a printer who found it contained 'obscene' words and who took it to the police. Merely taking the manuscript to the printer was judged to be 'publishing an obscene libel'. The case was taken to the Court of Criminal Appeal where the judges were aware that the defence was being paid for by such men as T. S. Eliot, Laurence Housman, Aldous Huxley, Walter de la Mare, J. B. Priestley, H. G. Wells and Hugh Walpole, but the conviction was upheld (see *Books in the Dock* (London, André Deutsch, 1969)).
5. Harrison read some passages from the book to an assembly of journalists in Canberra and while he was reading the Minister for External Affairs, Sir Frederick Stewart, walked into the room. 'Words fail me', he said, 'I have not a sufficiently wide vocabulary to express my opinion of this book.' Peter Coleman, who reports these events in his *Obscenity, Blasphemy, Sedition* (Sydney, Angus and Robertson, 1974), adds that Sir Frederick nevertheless made an attempt by describing it as 'a collection of unadulterated filth'.
6. Cited in *Pornography: the Longford Report*, p. 114.
7. *Ibid*. p. 201.
8. 'Moral protectionism' in G. Dutton and M. Harris (eds.), *Australia's Censorship Crisis* (Melbourne, Sun Books, 1970).

9. *Ibid.* pp. 99–103.
10. 'Obscenity as an aesthetic category', *Law and Contemporary Problems*, vol. 20, no. 4 (Autumn 1955).
11. *Ibid.* p. 134.
12. *The Use of Poetry and the Use of Criticism* (London, Faber and Faber, 1933), p. 30.
13. *The Fire and the Sun* (Oxford, Clarendon Press, 1977), pp. 83–6.
14. See F. R. Leavis, *Revaluation* (London, Chatto and Windus, 1962), pp. 29–30 for a development of this point.
15. John Casey, *The Language of Criticism* (London, Methuen, 1966), p. 183.
16. 'It is certainly the case that when a man habitually expresses his feelings at the level of banal and sentimental cliché there are important categories of emotional seriousness we cannot attribute to him. He lacks the capacity to have certain feelings just insofar as he lacks the mastery of certain forms of verbal expression. There is no question of separating the thing said from the manner of saying it' (*ibid.* p. 189).
17. There is a sense in which poems often do seem to 'recommend attitudes'. My argument will be that 'recommend' is mistaken. Attitudes are presented/enacted/dramatized, not recommended.
18. For example, feminist novels may convince us that our view of the role of women in society is chauvinistic.
19. *The Language of Criticism*, p. 183.
20. See above, p. 15.
21. In Casey's sense of the term.
22. *The Longford Report*, p. 202.
23. Charles Rembar, the defence lawyer at the American trial of *Lady Chatterley's Lover*, points out that 'right up to 1966 some judges denounced good writing on the ground that it made a pernicious book all the more effective' (*The End of Obscenity* (London, André Deutsch, 1969), p. 24).
24. D. H. Lawrence, 'Morality and the novel', *Phoenix*, ed. E. D. McDonald (London, Heinemann, 1936), pp. 532 and 528.
25. D. H. Lawrence, 'Why the novel matters', *Phoenix*, p. 534.
26. See above, p. 107.
27. Arguments which support free expression of whatever kind depend on more general considerations concerning liberty – see, for example, J. S. Mill *On Liberty*.
28. Cf. my earlier example of the teacher in the police college who dealt with *Romeo and Juliet* as a study in juvenile delinquency.
29. Roth describes his unsent letter as 'an example of a flourishing subliterary genre with a long and moving history'. His reasons for not posting the letter are 'the reasons why such letters rarely are mailed, or written for that matter, other than in the novelist's skull'.

   1. Writing (or imagining writing) the letter is sufficiently cathartic: by 4 or 5 a.m. the dispute has usually been settled to the novelist's satisfaction, and he can turn over and get a few hours sleep.

2. It is unlikely that the critic is about to have his reading corrected by the novelist anyway.

3. One does not want to appear piqued in the least – let alone to be seething – neither to the critic nor to the public that follows these duels when they are conducted out in the open for all to see.

4. Where is it engraved in stone that a novelist shall feel himself to be 'understood' any better than anyone else does?

5. The advice of friends and loved ones 'For God's sake, forget it.'

> (*Reading Myself and Others* (London, Corgi, 1977), p. 21)

30. *Ibid.* pp. 26–8.
31. *Ibid.* p. 25.
32. Donald Davie, *Shenandoah* (20 Feb. 1978), 47.
33. *The Melbourne Critical Review*, no. 6 (1963), 32.
34. Cf. once again Eliot's observation that the author's experience is 'ordered in some way which may be very different from the way of valuation of practical life'.
35. *Melbourne Critical Review*, 40.

Index

Index

honesty of untutored response, 43
Hopkins, G. M., 145
Hough, Graham, 59–60
Housman, A. E., 144–5
Hume, David, 72–3, 113

identification with fictional characters, 5, 109, 110, 112, 114–16
imagery, 50–3
imagined experience, entertained by poet, 58; realized in poem, 60–1
indoctrination, 97–9; distinguished from education, 99; teaching of values seen as, 96
inner life, writing as access to, 12
insincerity, in art, 10–12; of art, 8–9
integrity, 22
intention of author, 5–6, 30
intuitive understanding and empathy, 121–4
involvement with fictional personages, 3, 4, 5; see also identification
ironia, 128
irony, 8, 9–10

Jakobson, Roman, 93, 94
James, Henry, *The Art of Fiction*, 44; author's intention, 136, 137; Culler on, 84; integration of literary work, 57; relation between aspects of the novel, 44; *The Turn of the Screw*, 136, 137; Wilson, Edmund, on, 136, 137; *The Wings of the Dove*, 84
'Jerusalem', 143
Johnson, Lionel, 53
Johnson, Samuel, 133
Jong, Erica, 7–8, 10–12, 14, 22, 45
Joyce, James, 5, 150
judgements, nature of literary, 15–19; see also criticism; value judgements

Kaplan, Abraham, 152, 153
Keats, John, 51–2, 54–6
Kettle, Arnold, 45–6
knowledge of life through literature, 12
Kristeva, Julia, 79

Lady Chatterley's Lover, trial of, 5, 150
Language of Criticism, The, 1
Langer, Susanne K., 103–4
Lawrence, D. H., artist not to be trusted, 135; interrelatedness of the novel, 44; Leavis on, 52; novel's relevance to life, 156–7; operative intention in novels, 147; 'Piano', 52; views of author and his characters, 147
Leavis, F. R., appreciation of literature must be personal, 42–3; on Blake, 50–1; critical concepts for poetry, 50–4; definition of 'realization', 56–7; dialectical reasoning in criticism, 70–1; on Donne, 55; *Education and the University*, 56; enactment, 54–8; evaluation as critic's aim, 102; on Keats, 51–2, 54; on Marvell, 154; on Shakespeare, 37–8; nature of his critical reasoning, 37–8, 49–53; relation between literature and reality, 58–61
Lesser, Simon O., 109
life, knowledge of through literature, 12; literature as substitute for, 125; literature in relation to, 2–6
literary criticism, see criticism
literary judgement, personal preference in, 63–74; uncertainty in, 66–7
Litz, Walton, 47
Lodge, David, 93–4
Lolita, 4, 130
Longford Committee Investigating Pornography, 150–1, 156
'Love Song of J. Alfred Prufrock, The', 141
Lysistrata, 150

Macbeth, 25–6, 37–8
Macdonald, Margaret, 64–5
Mace, C. A., 100
Martin, Jane, 121–3
Marvell, Christopher, 36, 53, 141, 159–61
matter and style, see form and content
meaning, author's and reader's, 133, 134–5; rather than mere existence, of works of literature, 68
metaphysical poetry, Leavis on, 53
Meynell, Hugo, 73
Miller, Hillis, 87
Milton, John, 135, 145

mimesis, literature as, 8
Montgomerie, John, 156
moral danger of literature, 2, 5–6, 126; see also obscenity
moral education through literature, 4–5
moral neutrality of art, 9
Mounce, H. O., 104, 105, 106–8
'movement' in poetry, 51–3
Murdoch, Iris, danger of illusion in art, 8–10; literature reflecting life, 15, 155; on Plato, 8–10, 11; truth in art, 8–10, 11, 14, 15
Murray, W. A., 95

Nabokov, Vladimir, 4, 130
'New' New Criticism, 90–1
Nixon, Richard (President), on obscenity, 150
'Nocturnall on S. Lucies Day', 128
non-verbal experience, 21–31
Northanger Abbey, 114–19
novel, organic nature of, 44–8

objective existence of works of literature, 68
objectives of schooling, 98–9
objectivity, and infallibility, 64–5; and intelligibility, 64–5
obscenity, 5, 156, 153
Oliver Twist, 45–6
organic nature of novel, 44–8

Paradise Lost, 135, 145
parallel cases, reasoning from, 75–6
Peacock, R., 71, 73–5
Perry, L. R., 2
Persuasion, 46–7
Peters, R. S., 100
Plato, 2, 5, 8–11, 15, 113, 151
playfulness of art, 154
pleasure principle as motivation for reading fiction, 109–12
plot in the novel, 45–6
poetics, Jonathan Culler's, 77–87
Poole, Roger, 86
Pope, Alexander, 18–19, 26
pornography, 5, 152
Portnoy's Complaint, 158–9; trial of, 5
Psycho, 106, 135
pulp novels and stereotyping, 130

realism about material world, and objectivity, 65–6
realism in literature, psychological purpose of, 104–6, 109–11
reality, in art, 15–16; principle in fiction, 111–12; relation to literature, 13–15, 21
realization, 30–1, Leavis' definition of, 56–7
Reid, L. A., 33–4, 35, 40–1
Ricks, Christopher, 88–9
Romeo and Juliet, 5
Roth, Philip, 158–9

Scheffler, Israel, 120
School of Venus, The, 152
schooling, mass competitive, effects of, 42
Schools Council Research Study, 108–13, 114–19
scientific judgements, contrasted with literary judgements, 64–5
Scriven, Michael, 69–70
Secret Agent, The, 114
semiotics, 79; semiology, Culler's poetics, 77–87
sensitivity to literature, 119–20
sentimentality, 126
Shakespeare, William, 63, *Antony and Cleopatra*, 3, 4, 67, 129, 155; *King Lear*, 84, 104–6; *Macbeth*, 25–6, 37–8; *Romeo and Juliet*, 5
Shelley, Percy Bysshe, 50–1; Culler on 'The Cloud', 81–2
Sibley, F. N., 67, 68
sincerity in literature, 12
Stevens, Wallace, 82
Stolnitz, J., 13, 34
Structuralism and Semiotics, 90
Structuralist Poetics, 77–9
substance and style, see form and content

television and escapism, 117, 127
Tennyson, Alfred, Lord, 52, 58–60